Easter
by Emma J. Lee
Everything You Need To Know
About Lent and Easter

- A New Zealand Made Product

Get A Free Book At: BornIncredible.com/free-book-offer/[4]

1. https://BornIncredible.com
2. https://BornIncredible.com
3. https://BornIncredible.com
4. **https://bornincredible.com/free-book-offer/**

Introduction

Easter is one of the most significant and widely celebrated holidays around the world. For Christians, it commemorates the resurrection of Jesus Christ, an event that holds a central place in the faith. However, Easter is more than just a religious holiday. It is a time of renewal, hope, and new beginnings, celebrated by people of all faiths and cultures.

In this book, we will explore the history, significance, and traditions of Easter, from the ancient pagan roots to modern-day celebrations. We will examine the biblical accounts of the events leading up to the resurrection of Jesus Christ, as well as the customs and practices associated with the holiday.

We will also take a closer look at the meaning of Lent, a period of fasting, prayer, and reflection that precedes Easter. We will explore the spiritual significance of Lenten practices, such as fasting and abstaining, prayer and meditation, and acts of social justice and charity.

Moreover, we will delve into the various Easter symbols and traditions, including the Easter egg, the Easter bunny, and the custom of decorating Easter baskets. We will also explore the ways in which Easter is celebrated around the world, from the liturgical customs of the Christian faith to the secular observances of the holiday.

Ultimately, this book aims to provide a comprehensive guide to the Easter holiday, examining its religious and cultural significance, as well as the various customs and traditions that have developed around it over the centuries. Whether you are a devout Christian, a curious explorer of cultures and religions, or simply someone looking to learn more about this beloved holiday, this book is for you.

The Start of Easter

Easter is a holiday with religious significance for Christians around the world, but it also has a history rooted in pagan traditions. Many ancient cultures celebrated the spring equinox, which occurs around March 20th, as a time of rebirth and renewal. In fact, the word "Easter" itself comes from the Old English word "ēastre," which was the name of a pagan goddess associated with spring and fertility.

As Christianity spread throughout Europe, early Christians sought to convert pagans by incorporating their existing beliefs and traditions into Christian practices. One way this was done was by aligning the Christian celebration of Jesus' resurrection with the pagan celebration of the spring equinox.

Over time, many of the pagan symbols and practices associated with the spring equinox were adapted to fit within the context of the Christian Easter holiday. For example, the egg, which was a symbol of fertility and new life in many pagan cultures, came to represent the empty tomb of Jesus after his resurrection.

While Easter has retained many of its pagan roots, it is primarily celebrated as a Christian holiday commemorating the resurrection of Jesus. However, the blending of religious and secular traditions has made Easter a beloved holiday celebrated by many people around the world, regardless of their religious beliefs.

Easter Religious significance

Easter is a significant event in the Christian calendar, marking the celebration of the resurrection of Jesus Christ. This holiday holds a deep spiritual significance for Christians around the world, as it represents the triumph of life over death and the promise of eternal life.

The history of Easter can be traced back to the Jewish celebration of Passover, which commemorates the liberation of the Israelites from slavery in ancient Egypt. It was during the Passover celebration that Jesus was arrested, tried, and sentenced to death by crucifixion.

Following his death, Jesus was buried in a tomb, where he remained for three days before rising from the dead. This miraculous event is celebrated as Easter, which is observed on the first Sunday after the first full moon following the spring equinox.

For Christians, Easter is a time of reflection, renewal, and rejoicing. It is a time to remember the sacrifice that Jesus made and to celebrate the hope and promise of eternal life that his resurrection represents. It is also a time to come together as a community and to share in the joy and fellowship of the season.

Over the centuries, Easter has become an important part of the cultural and religious traditions of many nations around the world. From the colorful parades and festive meals of Latin America to the solemn church services and symbolic egg hunts of Europe and North America, Easter is a time for people of all ages and backgrounds to come together and celebrate the renewal of life and hope that this holiday represents.

The Biblical Basis for Easter

Easter is the celebration of the resurrection of Jesus Christ from the dead, and is the most significant event in the Christian calendar. The story of Easter begins with the events leading up to the crucifixion of Jesus.

Jesus arrived in Jerusalem on Palm Sunday, where he was greeted by crowds waving palm branches and laying them on the ground in front of him. This was seen as a sign of respect and honor, and was a common practice for dignitaries in that time. Jesus spent the next few days in the city, teaching and preaching to the people.

On Thursday of that week, Jesus celebrated the Passover meal with his disciples. During the meal, he predicted that one of his disciples would betray him. Later that evening, Jesus was betrayed by Judas and arrested by the Roman authorities.

The following day, Jesus was brought before Pilate, the Roman governor of Judea. Despite finding no fault with Jesus, Pilate was pressured by the Jewish leaders and ordered that Jesus be crucified.

Jesus was taken to a hill outside the city and was crucified, which was a common form of execution in the Roman Empire.

After Jesus died on the cross, his body was placed in a tomb. On the third day, Sunday, Mary Magdalene and other women went to the tomb to anoint Jesus' body. When they arrived, they found that the stone covering the entrance to the tomb had been rolled away, and the tomb was empty.

According to the Gospels, Jesus then appeared to his disciples over a period of forty days, performing miracles and teaching them before ascending into heaven. This event is known as the resurrection, and is considered by Christians to be proof of Jesus' divinity and the promise of eternal life.

The resurrection of Jesus is central to the Christian faith, and is celebrated every year at Easter. Easter is a time for reflection and renewal, and a time to remember the sacrifice that Jesus made for humanity.

Easter in the Bible

Easter, also known as Resurrection Sunday, is a Christian holiday that celebrates the resurrection of Jesus Christ from the dead. As such, the events of Easter are an integral part of the New Testament, particularly the Gospels of Matthew, Mark, Luke, and John.

The Gospel of Matthew tells of Mary Magdalene and the other Mary who went to Jesus' tomb on the morning after the Sabbath. There they discovered that the stone had been rolled away and the tomb was empty. Suddenly an angel appeared and told them that Jesus had risen from the dead. The women then went to tell the disciples the good news.

In the Gospel of Mark, the women found the tomb already open when they arrived. They went inside and found a young man dressed in white who told them that Jesus had risen from the dead and was going ahead of them to Galilee. The women were afraid and fled from the tomb, but eventually told the disciples what they had seen.

In the Gospel of Luke, the women went to the tomb with spices to anoint Jesus' body. When they arrived, they found the stone had been rolled away and the tomb was empty. Two men in dazzling clothes appeared and told the women that Jesus had risen from the dead. The women returned and told the disciples what they had seen, but the disciples did not believe them.

In the Gospel of John, Mary Magdalene went to the tomb and found it empty. She ran to tell the disciples, who then went to see for themselves. Later, Jesus appeared to his disciples, including Thomas, who had doubted the resurrection until he saw Jesus in person.

The meaning of Easter in Christian theology is that through his death and resurrection, Jesus conquered sin and death and made it possible for all people to have eternal life. Easter is therefore a celebration of hope, renewal, and new beginnings for Christians around the world.

Easter Traditions and Celebrations

Easter is a festival that is associated with several symbols and traditions that have been celebrated for centuries. In this chapter, we will explore some of the most well-known Easter symbols and traditions and the stories behind them.

The Easter Egg

Easter eggs are a universal symbol of Easter. They are believed to have been used in the celebration of Easter since the early Christian era. The egg represents new life and resurrection, making it a fitting symbol for Easter.

In many cultures, eggs are dyed or painted in bright colors and patterns, and are used in Easter egg hunts and as gifts. In some cultures, Easter eggs are decorated with religious motifs, such as crosses and other religious symbols.

History of the Easter Egg

The tradition of the Easter egg can be traced back to ancient civilizations, including the Greeks, Persians, and Egyptians. These cultures saw the egg as a symbol of new life and rebirth, particularly in the context of springtime and the changing of seasons.

In Christian tradition, the Easter egg is often associated with the resurrection of Jesus Christ. In the early days of Christianity, eggs were dyed red to represent the blood of Christ shed during the crucifixion. The shell of the egg, which represents the tomb of Christ, was then cracked open to symbolize his resurrection from the dead.

Over time, the tradition of coloring and decorating Easter eggs became more elaborate, with different cultures developing their own unique styles and techniques. In some parts of Europe, for example, elaborate designs were created using wax and dyes to create intricate patterns on the eggs.

Today, the Easter egg remains a beloved symbol of the holiday, with many families incorporating the tradition of coloring and decorating eggs as part of their Easter celebrations.

The Easter Bunny

The Easter Bunny is another popular Easter symbol. The Easter Bunny is believed to have its roots in Germanic folklore, where it was a symbol of fertility and new life. The tradition of the Easter Bunny was brought to America by German immigrants in the 18th century.

In many cultures, the Easter Bunny is associated with the delivery of Easter eggs to children. The Easter Bunny is often depicted as a cute, fluffy animal with long ears and a cotton tail.

History of the Easter bunny

The Easter bunny is a popular symbol of Easter, particularly in Western cultures, and is often associated with the delivery of Easter eggs and candy to children. The origins of the Easter bunny, however, are not entirely clear and have been the subject of much debate.

One theory is that the Easter bunny originated in Germany in the 16th century, where it was known as the "Osterhase" or "Oschter Haws." According to this theory, the Osterhase was a hare that laid colored eggs for children to find on Easter morning. The tradition was brought to America by German immigrants in the 18th and 19th centuries.

Another theory suggests that the Easter bunny may have its roots in pre-Christian pagan traditions. In some pagan cultures, the rabbit or hare was a symbol of fertility and new life, which are themes also associated with the Christian celebration of Easter.

Regardless of its origins, the Easter bunny has become a beloved symbol of Easter in many parts of the world. In addition to delivering Easter eggs and candy, the Easter bunny is often depicted as a friendly and playful creature, and is a popular subject for Easter-themed crafts and decorations.

Other Easter Symbols and Their Meanings

Easter lilies, white doves, and the Paschal candle are other symbols that are often associated with Easter. The Easter lily, with its pure white color, is seen as a symbol of the resurrection of Christ. The white dove is a symbol of peace and is often used to represent the Holy Spirit. The Paschal candle is lit during Easter services and represents the risen Christ.

Easter Traditions Around the World

Easter is celebrated in many different ways around the world. In some countries, such as Greece and Russia, Easter is a bigger holiday than Christmas. In other countries, such as the United States and the United Kingdom, Easter is celebrated with Easter egg hunts and visits from the Easter Bunny.

In Mexico and other Latin American countries, Easter is celebrated with the reenactment of the crucifixion of Jesus. In Sweden, children dress up as Easter witches and go from house to house, exchanging drawings and paintings for sweets.

Overall, the symbols and traditions of Easter have been celebrated for centuries and continue to be an important part of the Easter holiday.

The Easter Season

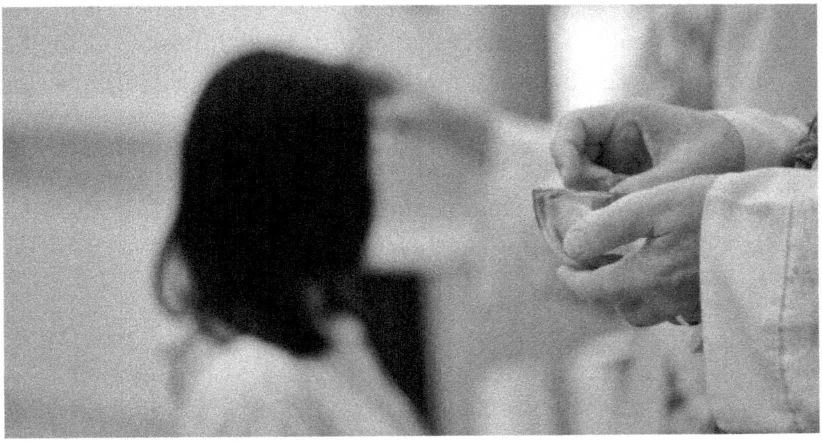

The Easter Season is a significant period in the Christian calendar that encompasses several days leading up to and following the celebration of Easter. The Easter Season begins with the season of Lent, which starts on Ash Wednesday and lasts for forty days, during which Christians prepare themselves for the Easter celebration.

Holy Week is the week leading up to Easter and is considered one of the most important weeks in the Christian calendar. Holy Week begins with Palm Sunday, commemorating Jesus' triumphal entry into Jerusalem. Maundy Thursday marks the Last Supper of Jesus and his disciples, during which he instituted the Eucharist. Good Friday is the day when Jesus was crucified, and it is observed as a day of solemn reflection and mourning. Holy Saturday is the day that Jesus lay in the tomb, and it is a time of quiet waiting and preparation for the celebration of Easter.

The celebration of Easter marks the resurrection of Jesus Christ from the dead, which is a fundamental tenet of the Christian faith. It is a joyful celebration of new life, hope, and renewal. Easter is typically celebrated on the first Sunday following the first full moon after the vernal equinox. The season of Easter, which lasts for fifty days, is a time of rejoicing and celebration of the resurrection.

Throughout the Easter Season, Christians participate in various traditions and observances that reflect the significance of the Easter story. These can include attending church services, reading scripture, praying, and engaging in acts of service and charity.

Easter is a time of celebration and renewal, and it offers a reminder of the hope and promise of new life that is at the heart of the Christian faith.

Lent

Lent is a period of preparation for the Christian celebration of Easter. It is observed in many Christian denominations, including Catholic, Orthodox, Anglican, and Protestant churches. The season of Lent begins on Ash Wednesday, which is 46 days before Easter, and lasts until Holy Saturday, the day before Easter.

What is Lent?

Lent is a period of spiritual reflection and discipline. During this time, Christians are encouraged to repent, pray, and give alms. The word "lent" comes from the Old English word "lencten," which means "springtime." Lent is a time of spiritual growth and renewal, much like the spring season.

The history of Lent

The origins of Lent can be traced back to the early Christian church. In the second century, Christians observed a period of fasting and penance in preparation for Easter. This period of preparation varied in length and practice throughout the early church. It wasn't until the Council of Nicaea in 325 AD that the length of Lent was officially set at 40 days, in commemoration of Jesus' 40-day fast in the wilderness.

The role of Lent in various Christian traditions

Lent is observed in many Christian denominations, but the practices and customs vary. In the Catholic Church, Lent is a time of penance, fasting, and abstinence. Catholics are asked to abstain from meat on Ash Wednesday and all Fridays during Lent. They are also encouraged to give up something that is important to them, such as a favorite food or activity.

In the Orthodox Church, Lent is known as the Great Lent and lasts for 40 days. Orthodox Christians are asked to fast during the entire period, abstaining from meat, dairy, and other animal products.

Protestant denominations also observe Lent, although the practices and customs vary. Some Protestant churches encourage fasting or giving up something during Lent, while others do not.

Sundays during Lent

Sundays are not traditionally counted as part of the 40-day period of Lent. This is because Sundays are considered "mini-Easters" that celebrate the resurrection of Jesus, and thus they are days of joy and not of mourning or penance. In essence, Sundays are meant to break the fasting and abstinence routines of Lent, and allow for a time of celebration and reflection on the core beliefs of Christianity. While Lent is a season of sacrifice, it is also a time of spiritual growth, and Sundays are seen as an opportunity to renew one's faith and recommit to the practices of Lent.

Lent is a period of spiritual growth and renewal for Christians. It is a time to reflect on one's faith, repent, and prepare for the celebration of Easter. The history and significance of Lent are deeply rooted in Christian tradition, and it continues to be observed in many denominations today. Whether it involves fasting, prayer, or other spiritual practices, Lent is an important time for Christians to deepen their relationship with God and with one another.

The Meaning of Lent

Lent is a period of fasting, reflection, and preparation that begins on Ash Wednesday and ends on Holy Saturday. For Christians, it is a time of spiritual renewal and preparation for the celebration of Easter. Lent is observed by many denominations, including Catholics, Orthodox Christians, and many Protestant denominations.

The purpose of Lent is to deepen one's faith through self-examination, prayer, and acts of charity. The period of Lent is based on the 40 days that Jesus spent in the wilderness, where he fasted and prayed before beginning his ministry. Lent is therefore a time to follow in the footsteps of Jesus, to focus on our relationship with God, and to reflect on our spiritual journey.

Lenten practices often include fasting, which means to abstain from food or certain types of food for a period of time. Fasting is a way of denying oneself to focus more intently on spiritual matters. Prayer is also an important part of Lent, and many people choose to spend more time in prayer or to engage in specific types of prayer such as the Rosary or Stations of the Cross. Acts of charity, such as giving to the poor or volunteering at a local shelter, are also common practices during Lent.

The connection between Lent and the life of Jesus is central to the observance of this season. During Lent, Christians focus on the life, death, and resurrection of Jesus. This includes reading the Gospels, attending special services, and meditating on the passion of Christ.

The theological significance of Lenten disciplines is rooted in the belief that we are called to follow Christ and to imitate his life. Through the practices of prayer, fasting, and charity, we seek to become more like Christ and to deepen our relationship with God.

Lent is therefore a time of spiritual growth and renewal, a time to turn away from sin and to embrace the way of Christ.

In conclusion, the meaning of Lent is found in its practices, its connection to the life of Jesus, and its theological significance. Lent is a time to deepen our faith, to focus on our relationship with God, and to prepare ourselves for the celebration of Easter. Through prayer, fasting, and acts of charity, we seek to become more like Christ and to grow in our understanding of the Christian faith.

Lenten Practices

Lenten practices are an opportunity to reflect on the life and teachings of Jesus, and to grow in one's faith through spiritual disciplines.

One of the most common practices during Lent is fasting. Fasting involves limiting food intake or abstaining from certain types of food or drink. This practice is meant to help individuals focus on their spiritual life, and to remind them of their dependence on God. Fasting can take many forms, such as giving up meat on Fridays, abstaining from sweets, or skipping meals altogether.

Abstaining from something during Lent is another popular practice. This can include abstaining from social media, television, or other distractions that can take away from one's spiritual life. By abstaining from something, individuals create space for prayer, meditation, and other spiritual practices.

Prayer and meditation are important practices during Lent. Many people use this time to read the Bible or other spiritual literature, spend time in silent reflection, or attend prayer services. Prayer can take many forms, including petition, intercession, thanksgiving, and praise. Meditation involves quieting the mind and focusing on a particular thought or Scripture passage.

Almsgiving and social justice are also important Lenten practices. Almsgiving involves giving to those in need, whether through financial donations or volunteering time. Social justice involves addressing the root causes of poverty, inequality, and injustice. This can involve advocating for policy changes, volunteering with organizations that work with vulnerable populations, or supporting fair trade products.

Other Lenten practices and disciplines include attending Mass, participating in the Stations of the Cross, making a pilgrimage, or studying the lives of the saints. The goal of these practices is to draw closer to God, to repent of one's sins, and to prepare for the celebration of Easter.

In summary, Lenten practices are an opportunity to deepen one's faith and grow in relationship with God. Fasting, abstaining, prayer, meditation, and other practices can help individuals reflect on the life and teachings of Jesus, and to prepare for the celebration of Easter. These practices can be challenging, but they can also be rewarding, as they lead to spiritual growth and transformation.

The Journey of Lent

Lent is a period of reflection and preparation in the Christian faith, observed by various denominations including Roman Catholics, Eastern Orthodox, Anglicans, and Lutherans. It is a 40-day period of spiritual discipline, culminating in Holy Week and Easter Sunday. The season of Lent is intended to be a time of self-examination and self-discipline, as believers reflect on their faith and seek to grow closer to God.

The liturgical calendar of Lent begins on Ash Wednesday and concludes on Easter Sunday, with Holy Week being the most significant part of the season. During Holy Week, the final week of Lent, believers commemorate the events leading up to Jesus' crucifixion and resurrection.

The significance of the Lenten journey lies in its focus on repentance, humility, and spiritual renewal. Believers are encouraged to fast, pray, and practice other forms of self-denial as a way of detaching from worldly concerns and drawing closer to God. Lent is a time to reflect on one's own shortcomings and to seek forgiveness for sins.

The Triduum, which means "three days," is the period between the evening of Holy Thursday and the evening of Easter Sunday. The Triduum is the most important part of the Christian liturgical year, and is marked by a series of religious services and observances. These include the Mass of the Lord's Supper on Holy Thursday, the Veneration of the Cross on Good Friday, and the Easter Vigil on Holy Saturday. The Triduum culminates in the celebration of Easter Sunday, the day of Jesus' resurrection.

In conclusion, the Lenten journey is a time of spiritual growth and renewal, marked by a period of self-reflection and discipline. It is an opportunity for believers to draw closer to God and to deepen their understanding of the life and teachings of Jesus. The Triduum and Easter Sunday are the culmination of this journey, marking the celebration of the resurrection and the hope that it brings to all who believe.

Ash Wednesday

Ash Wednesday is a Christian holy day that marks the beginning of Lent, a 40-day period of prayer, fasting, and repentance in preparation for the celebration of Easter. It is observed by many Western Christian denominations, including Roman Catholic, Anglican, and Lutheran churches, and is traditionally held on the Wednesday following the seventh Sunday before Easter.

On Ash Wednesday, many Christians attend a special church service, during which they receive ashes on their foreheads in the shape of a cross. The ashes are made by burning palm fronds that were blessed on the previous year's Palm Sunday. The imposition of ashes is accompanied by the words "Remember that you are dust, and to dust you shall return," a reminder of the mortality of human life and the need for spiritual renewal.

The history of Ash Wednesday can be traced back to the early Christian Church, when penitents would be publicly marked with ashes as a sign of their repentance. The practice was later incorporated into the liturgy of the Church and has been observed in various forms ever since.

In addition to receiving ashes, many Christians observe a period of fasting, prayer, and other spiritual practices during Lent as a way of preparing themselves for the celebration of Easter. This can include abstaining from certain foods or activities, attending daily worship services, or engaging in acts of service and charity.

The observance of Ash Wednesday and Lent serves as a reminder of the need for repentance and renewal in the Christian life, and as an opportunity to deepen one's relationship with God. It is a time for reflection, introspection, and spiritual growth, and an invitation to all Christians to draw closer to the divine presence.

Lent in Different Christian Traditions

The observance of Lent can vary greatly between different Christian denominations, and even within the same denomination. In the Roman Catholic Church, Lent begins on Ash Wednesday and lasts for 40 days, representing the 40 days Jesus spent fasting in the desert before beginning his ministry. The focus is on repentance and self-denial, with practices such as fasting, abstinence, and acts of charity. Eastern Orthodox Christians observe Lent for 40 days as well, but begin the observance on Clean Monday, the first day of Lent. They also abstain from meat and dairy products for the duration of Lent, and may have different fasting and prayer practices.

In Protestant denominations, the observance of Lent varies, with some following a similar practice to the Roman Catholic Church, and others not observing it at all. Many Anglican and Episcopal churches observe Lent, with a focus on prayer, fasting, and works of mercy. Some Baptist and evangelical churches may not have a formal observance of Lent, but may encourage their members to give up something for the season or practice daily devotionals.

Customs and practices for Lent can also vary between cultures. In some countries, it is traditional to give up meat for the entire 40-day period, while in others, it is common to only abstain on Fridays. Some cultures have unique practices, such as the Spanish tradition of Semana Santa, or Holy Week, which includes processions and reenactments of the passion of Christ.

The significance of Lent in global Christianity is that it is a time of spiritual preparation for the celebration of Easter, which is the most important Christian holiday. It is a time for reflection, repentance, and self-denial, with a focus on deepening one's relationship with God. The practices of Lent, such as fasting and prayer, help Christians to be more mindful of their faith and to develop a deeper sense of humility and gratitude.

In conclusion, Lent is an important observance in the Christian faith, with a variety of practices and customs that can vary greatly between cultures and traditions. The significance of Lent is in its focus on spiritual preparation for the celebration of Easter, with a focus on repentance, self-denial, and deepening one's relationship with God.

Reflection and Renewal

Lent is a time of spiritual reflection and renewal observed in many Christian traditions around the world. During this 40-day period leading up to Easter, believers engage in various practices and disciplines that help them deepen their relationship with God and prepare for the celebration of Jesus' resurrection.

The purpose of Lenten practices is to help us focus on our spiritual life and grow closer to God. Fasting, abstaining from certain foods, and giving up something we enjoy are common disciplines during this season. These practices help us to acknowledge our reliance on God, reflect on our blessings, and become more disciplined in our lives.

The connection between Lent and the life of Jesus is profound. Lent represents the time that Jesus spent in the desert, fasting and praying, before he began his public ministry. During Lent, Christians reflect on the temptations that Jesus faced in the desert and the sacrifices that he made for our salvation. This reflection helps us to deepen our understanding of Jesus' life and mission and to appreciate the gift of salvation that he offers us.

The theological significance of Lenten disciplines is rooted in the belief that through our self-denial, prayer, and repentance, we can grow closer to God and become more Christlike. Lent is a time for personal reflection, examination of conscience, and spiritual growth. The disciplines of Lent help us to develop a greater awareness of our weaknesses and our need for God's grace and mercy.

Fasting and abstaining, prayer and meditation, and almsgiving and social justice are the primary Lenten practices. Fasting and abstaining help us to become more disciplined and self-controlled. Prayer and meditation help us to deepen our relationship with God and develop a more contemplative and prayerful spirit. Almsgiving and social justice help us to become more aware of the needs of others and to develop a spirit of compassion and generosity.

Other Lenten practices and disciplines include confession and reconciliation, spiritual reading and study, and participation in liturgical services. These practices help us to become more focused on our spiritual journey and to develop a greater sense of devotion and commitment to God.

The journey of Lent is marked by the liturgical calendar, which includes Ash Wednesday, the beginning of Lent, and Holy Week, which includes Palm Sunday, Maundy Thursday, Good Friday, and Holy Saturday. The significance of the Lenten journey is that it prepares us for the joyous celebration of Easter and the resurrection of Jesus.

The Triduum, which includes Holy Thursday, Good Friday, and Holy Saturday, is the most solemn time of the Lenten season. During this time, Christians reflect on the suffering and sacrifice of Jesus and prepare for the celebration of his resurrection. Easter is the culmination of the Lenten season and is a time of great joy and celebration.

Lent is observed in different Christian denominations and is accompanied by customs and practices that are unique to different cultures. Despite the differences, the significance of Lent in global Christianity is profound. Lent helps believers to deepen their relationship with God, develop a more disciplined and contemplative spirit, and become more compassionate and generous to others.

In conclusion, the season of Lent is a time of reflection and renewal that helps us to deepen our relationship with God and become more Christlike. Lenten practices and disciplines help us to become more disciplined, prayerful, and compassionate. The significance of Lent in global Christianity is profound and helps believers to grow in faith and devotion to God.

Significance of Lent

Lent is a season of spiritual preparation and renewal in the Christian faith. It is observed in various denominations, including Catholic, Orthodox, Anglican, and Lutheran, among others. The season of Lent begins on Ash Wednesday and lasts for forty days, not counting Sundays, culminating in Holy Week and Easter.

The purpose of Lenten practices is to focus on repentance, prayer, and spiritual discipline. Lent provides an opportunity for Christians to deepen their relationship with God and renew their commitment to living a life of faith. It is a time for reflection and introspection, as well as for giving back to those in need.

The connection between Lent and the life of Jesus is an essential part of the season. The forty days of Lent are symbolic of the forty days that Jesus spent in the wilderness before beginning his ministry. The Lenten disciplines of prayer, fasting, and almsgiving are modeled after Jesus' own spiritual practices, as well as those of the early Christian church.

The theological significance of Lenten disciplines is to help Christians prepare themselves for the celebration of Easter. Lenten disciplines create space for reflection, repentance, and renewal. Fasting and abstaining from certain foods or luxuries help Christians to focus on their spiritual needs rather than their physical desires. Prayer and meditation allow Christians to connect with God and seek guidance and strength. Almsgiving and social justice are practices that help Christians to live out their faith by serving others.

The most common Lenten practices include fasting and abstaining from meat on Ash Wednesday and on Fridays throughout the season. Fasting involves limiting food intake, while abstaining from meat symbolizes a sacrifice for spiritual purposes. Prayer and meditation are also vital Lenten practices that help Christians connect with God and seek guidance and support.

Almsgiving and social justice are also important Lenten practices. Almsgiving involves giving to those in need and making sacrifices to help others, while social justice involves advocating for the marginalized and seeking to make the world a more just and compassionate place.

Other Lenten practices and disciplines include attending daily Mass, participating in confession, and reading spiritual texts or devotionals. These practices help Christians to deepen their faith and grow in their relationship with God.

The significance of the Lenten journey is one of reflection and introspection. Christians are called to reflect on their lives and their relationship with God, seeking to repent of sin and grow in faith. The season of Lent culminates in Holy Week, which includes the celebration of Palm Sunday, Maundy Thursday, Good Friday, and Holy Saturday. These events lead to the celebration of Easter, which marks the resurrection of Jesus and the triumph of life over death.

The journey of Lent is significant in Christian traditions because it is a time for spiritual renewal and growth. The season of Lent provides a time for Christians to focus on their relationship with God, seeking to renew their faith and deepen their commitment to living a life of love and service.

Lent is observed in various Christian traditions around the world, including customs and practices that are unique to different cultures. The significance of Lent in global Christianity is the same, however, as it is a season of spiritual preparation and renewal that leads to the celebration of Easter.

In conclusion, the significance of Lent is the invitation to spiritual renewal and growth. Lenten practices help Christians to reflect on their lives, seek forgiveness and guidance from God, and renew their faith and commitment to living a life of love and service. The ongoing journey of faith beyond Lent is a continuing journey of reflection, renewal, and growth, leading to a deeper relationship with God and a life of meaning and purpose.

Holy Week History

Holy Week is the week leading up to Easter Sunday, commemorating the final days of Jesus' life, crucifixion, and resurrection. The events of Holy Week are recorded in the four Gospels of the New Testament, and the week is considered the most sacred time of the Christian calendar.

Holy Week begins on Palm Sunday, which marks the day when Jesus rode into Jerusalem on a donkey and was greeted by crowds waving palm branches. The day is also known as Passion Sunday, as it marks the beginning of the passion, or suffering, of Jesus leading up to his death.

The events of Holy Week continue on Maundy Thursday, which commemorates the Last Supper, where Jesus shared a final meal with his disciples and instituted the Eucharist. The name "Maundy" comes from the Latin word mandatum, which means "commandment," as Jesus gave his disciples the commandment to love one another as he had loved them.

Good Friday is the most solemn day of Holy Week, marking the day on which Jesus was crucified and died on the cross. Churches around the world hold services of solemn reflection and mourning on this day.

Holy Week culminates on Easter Sunday, which celebrates the resurrection of Jesus and the triumph of life over death. It is the most joyous day of the Christian calendar and is marked by church services, feasting, and the giving of Easter eggs and other gifts.

Palm Sunday: Jesus' Entrance into Jerusalem

Palm Sunday is a Christian celebration that takes place on the Sunday before Easter. It marks the beginning of Holy Week, which is the week leading up to Easter Sunday. Palm Sunday commemorates Jesus' entry into Jerusalem, which is described in the Bible as a triumphal procession.

According to the Gospel of John, Jesus rode into Jerusalem on a donkey, which was a symbol of peace. The people who had gathered to see him laid palm branches and their cloaks on the ground to make a path for him to pass through. They shouted, "Hosanna to the Son of David! Blessed is he who comes in the name of the Lord! Hosanna in the highest!"

This event is significant for Christians because it fulfilled an Old Testament prophecy that a king would enter Jerusalem on a donkey. It also marked the beginning of the end of Jesus' life on earth, as he knew that he was going to be arrested, tried, and crucified.

Today, many Christian churches celebrate Palm Sunday with processions of their own, in which congregants wave palm branches and sing hymns. Some churches also distribute palm fronds, which are used to make crosses and other religious symbols.

Palm Sunday is an important reminder of the humility and sacrifice of Jesus, and it serves as a powerful symbol of hope and redemption for Christians around the world.

Holy Wednesday – into the darkness

Holy Wednesday, also known as Spy Wednesday or Good Wednesday, is the Wednesday before Easter. In Christian tradition, it is the day on which Judas Iscariot betrayed Jesus for thirty pieces of silver. According to the Gospel accounts, Judas made a deal with the Sanhedrin to hand over Jesus in exchange for payment. This event led to Jesus' arrest and eventual crucifixion.

The name Spy Wednesday comes from the idea that Judas was acting as a spy on Jesus. The name Good Wednesday is used in some traditions because Jesus' actions on this day are seen as a preparation for his ultimate sacrifice on the cross.

In some Christian denominations, Holy Wednesday is marked by a Tenebrae service, which involves the gradual extinguishing of candles to symbolize the increasing darkness of Jesus' impending death. The service may also include readings from the Gospel accounts of the events leading up to the crucifixion.

Overall, Holy Wednesday is a somber day in the Christian calendar, reflecting on the betrayal of Judas and the impending death of Jesus.

Maundy Thursday – the Last Supper

Maundy Thursday, also known as Holy Thursday, is the day before Good Friday, which marks the crucifixion of Jesus. It is a significant day in the Christian faith and is the beginning of the Easter Triduum.

The name "Maundy Thursday" comes from the Latin word "mandatum," which means "commandment." It refers to the commandment that Jesus gave his disciples at the Last Supper to love one another as he had loved them.

The Last Supper is the meal that Jesus shared with his disciples on the night before he was arrested. During the meal, he washed the feet of his disciples as a symbol of his servitude, and he also broke bread and shared wine, telling his disciples that they were his body and blood.

Maundy Thursday is also significant because it marks the institution of the Eucharist, which is a central sacrament in the Christian faith. The Eucharist is the sharing of bread and wine, which is believed to represent the body and blood of Jesus.

In many churches, Maundy Thursday is celebrated with a special service in which the priest or pastor re-enacts the Last Supper, and the congregation shares in the Eucharist. Some churches also perform a foot-washing ceremony, in which the pastor or priest washes the feet of members of the congregation.

Maundy Thursday is a solemn and reflective day in the Christian faith, and it serves as a reminder of the sacrifice that Jesus made for humanity.

The Last Supper

The Last Supper is one of the most important events in the life of Jesus Christ, and is a key element of Christian tradition and theology. It is commonly believed to have taken place on the night before Jesus was crucified, during the Jewish festival of Passover.

During the Last Supper, Jesus shared bread and wine with his disciples, giving them new meaning as symbols of his body and blood. He also washed the feet of his disciples, teaching them the importance of humility and service.

The Last Supper has become an important symbol of Christian faith and is often depicted in art and literature. It is commemorated in Christian churches with the sacrament of Holy Communion, which involves the sharing of bread and wine in remembrance of Jesus' sacrifice.

The Last Supper is a powerful reminder of Jesus' teachings and the selfless sacrifice he made for humanity. It continues to inspire and guide Christians aro

und the world, and serves as a testament to the enduring power of faith and love.

The Eucharist

The Eucharist, also known as Holy Communion, is a central Christian sacrament that is often celebrated during church services, including on Maundy Thursday. The Eucharist involves the consumption of bread and wine that is believed to represent the body and blood of Jesus Christ. The practice of the Eucharist has its roots in the Last Supper, which Jesus shared with his disciples before his crucifixion. The symbolism of the bread and wine represents the sacrifice that Jesus made for humanity's sins and the hope of eternal life that his sacrifice offers. The Eucharist is a deeply spiritual and symbolic practice for many Christians, and is considered an important way to connect with Jesus and express faith in his message.

Good Friday – Jesus' agony on the cross

The origins of the name "Good Friday" are uncertain. Some believe that it is a corruption of the phrase "God's Friday," while others suggest that it may have been derived from the Middle English word "goode," meaning "holy." Still, others believe that it may have been a reference to the idea of "good" as a synonym for "pious" or "devout."

The first recorded use of the term "Good Friday" dates back to the 13th century, although it did not come into widespread use until the 16th century. The name is used in English-speaking countries, but other languages have different names for the day, such as "Karfreitag" (Sorrowful Friday) in German and "Viernes Santo" (Holy Friday) in Spanish.

Good Friday is the Friday before Easter Sunday and is a significant day in the Christian calendar. Good Friday marks the day of the crucifixion of Jesus Christ, and it is a day of solemn observance and mourning for Christians around the world.

Good Friday is typically observed with church services, prayer, and fasting, and many Christians will attend a special service to commemorate the crucifixion of Jesus. The service usually includes readings from the Gospels, prayers, and hymns, and may also include the traditional stations of the cross, which depict the events leading up to Jesus' crucifixion.

In some countries, such as the Philippines, there are also processions and re-enactments of the crucifixion, with devotees taking on the role of Jesus and carrying a cross through the streets. Good Friday is a solemn day of reflection and remembrance for Christians, as they contemplate the sacrifice that Jesus made for humanity.

Good Friday is not a public holiday in many countries, although it is observed as a public holiday in some countries with a significant Christian population, such as the Philippines. In many countries, businesses and schools may close early or close for the day, and there may be restrictions on the sale of alcohol and other activities.

Holy Saturday

Holy Saturday is the day between Good Friday and Easter Sunday, and it is a time of waiting and anticipation for Christians around the world. This day is often associated with the practice of visiting the tomb of Jesus, as it was on this day that Jesus was laid to rest in the tomb before his resurrection on Easter Sunday.

The tomb of Jesus is a significant site for Christians, as it symbolizes the final resting place of their savior and the ultimate triumph of life over death. For many believers, visiting the tomb of Jesus is a way to pay their respects to the Son of God and to connect with their faith on a deeper level.

The act of visiting the tomb of Jesus on Holy Saturday can be a powerful and moving experience. It is a time to reflect on the sacrifice that Jesus made for humanity and to contemplate the meaning of his death and resurrection. Many people find that visiting the tomb of Jesus helps them to feel closer to God and to better understand the mysteries of faith.

In addition to visiting the tomb of Jesus, there are many other ways to observe Holy Saturday. Some people choose to fast or to spend the day in prayer and meditation. Others may attend church services or engage in acts of charity or service to others.

Whatever your preferred way of observing Holy Saturday may be, it is a time to pause and reflect on the profound meaning of Jesus' death and resurrection. By visiting the tomb of Jesus or engaging in other spiritual practices, you can deepen your connection to your faith and draw closer to God.

Easter Sunday

Easter Sunday is the most important day in the Christian calendar. It is the day when Christians celebrate the resurrection of Jesus Christ. Easter Sunday is always celebrated on the first Sunday after the first full moon following the vernal equinox.

The resurrection of Jesus is the cornerstone of the Christian faith, and Easter Sunday is the day when this event is celebrated. Christians believe that Jesus was crucified and buried on Good Friday, and that he rose from the dead on Easter Sunday, three days later.

Easter Sunday is a day of great joy and celebration for Christians around the world. It is a time for families to come together, for church services, and for feasting and fun.

One of the most popular traditions associated with Easter Sunday is the giving of Easter eggs. The egg is a symbol of new life, and giving eggs at Easter is a way of celebrating the resurrection of Jesus.

In many parts of the world, there are other Easter traditions that are observed. In some countries, it is customary to decorate eggs, bake special Easter breads, or prepare traditional Easter meals.

Easter Sunday is also an important day for many non-Christian communities. In many cultures, the arrival of spring is celebrated at this time of year, and there are many festivals and celebrations that take place.

Overall, Easter Sunday is a day of hope, renewal, and new beginnings. It is a time to reflect on the sacrifice of Jesus and the promise of eternal life.

Easter Monday:

Easter Monday is a Christian holiday that is celebrated the day after Easter Sunday. It is also known as "Bright Monday" or "Renewal Monday." In some countries, it is observed as a public holiday and is a day off work.

The origins of Easter Monday can be traced back to the early Christian church. It was believed that the celebration of Easter should last for a full week, known as the "Octave of Easter." The Monday following Easter Sunday was designated as the second day of this octave and was a continuation of the celebration.

In many Christian traditions, Easter Monday is a day for reflection and contemplation. It is a time to reflect on the resurrection of Jesus and its significance for believers. In some churches, the Easter liturgy is continued on this day, with special readings and hymns.

In many cultures, Easter Monday is a day for outdoor activities and games. In the United Kingdom, it is known as "Bank Holiday Monday," and many people take the day off work to enjoy picnics, walks in the countryside, and other outdoor activities. In some parts of Europe, such as Hungary and the Czech Republic, there are Easter Monday traditions that involve pouring water on friends and family members to symbolize cleansing and renewal.

In the United States, Easter Monday is not widely celebrated as a public holiday. However, some churches and communities hold special services and events to mark the day.

Overall, Easter Monday is a day of celebration, reflection, and renewal for Christians around the world. Whether it is observed as a public holiday or a day for personal contemplation, it is a time to reflect on the joy and hope of the Easter season.

Celebrating Easter

Easter church services and customs Secular Easter celebrations Easter foods and recipes Decorating for Easter

Easter is one of the most significant holidays in the Christian faith, commemorating the resurrection of Jesus Christ. It is celebrated in various ways around the world, both within and outside of religious communities. Here are some ways that people celebrate Easter:

Easter Church Services and Customs:

1. Easter Vigil: Many churches hold a vigil on the night before Easter Sunday, which begins in darkness and ends in light to symbolize the resurrection.
2. Sunrise Services: Some churches hold outdoor services at sunrise to celebrate the resurrection.
3. Easter Mass: Many churches have special Masses on Easter Sunday, which may include baptisms or confirmations.
4. Customs: Some churches have special customs on Easter, such as the lighting of the Paschal candle or the singing of the Exsultet.

Secular Easter Celebrations:

1. Easter Egg Hunts: Many families and communities hold Easter egg hunts for children.
2. Easter Parades: Some cities hold parades with Easter-themed floats and displays.
3. Easter Bonnets: In some places, people wear elaborate hats or bonnets on Easter.
4. Easter Bunny: The Easter Bunny, a character who delivers eggs and treats to children, has become a popular secular symbol of Easter.

Easter Foods and Recipes:

1. Ham: Many families serve ham as the main course for their Easter meal.
2. Eggs: Eggs are a traditional symbol of Easter, and many families dye and decorate eggs for the holiday.
3. Hot Cross Buns: These sweet buns with a cross on top are a traditional Easter treat in many cultures.
4. Lamb: In some cultures, lamb is a traditional Easter dish.

Decorating for Easter:

1. Easter Eggs: Decorated eggs are a common Easter decoration, whether they are displayed in a basket or hung on a tree.
2. Flowers: Spring flowers such as tulips, daffodils, and lilies are popular Easter decorations.
3. Easter Baskets: Many families fill baskets with candy and treats for their children on Easter.
4. Easter Trees: Some people decorate trees with Easter eggs or other spring-themed ornaments.

Overall, Easter is a time of joy and celebration, whether it is celebrated in a religious or secular context. It is a time to gather with loved ones, reflect on the significance of the holiday, and enjoy the traditions and customs that make Easter special.

The Significance of Easter Today

Easter is a significant celebration in the Christian calendar, marking the resurrection of Jesus Christ from the dead. However, its meaning and celebration extend beyond the Christian faith, with Easter being observed as a cultural and secular holiday in many parts of the world. In this article, we will explore the significance of Easter today, including its spiritual, cultural, and non-religious aspects.

The spiritual meaning of Easter for Christians

For Christians, Easter is a time to celebrate the resurrection of Jesus Christ, which signifies the triumph of life over death and hope over despair. The resurrection of Jesus is believed to be the ultimate expression of God's love and the fulfillment of the promise of salvation for humanity. The Easter season is a time for reflection, spiritual renewal, and a deepening of one's faith.

How Easter is celebrated by non-Christians

Even though Easter has its roots in Christianity, it is celebrated by many people who do not identify as Christians. In many cultures, Easter has become a time for family gatherings, feasting, and the exchange of gifts. Easter eggs, Easter bunnies, and other symbols have become part of the secular celebration of Easter. The timing of Easter, which falls on the first Sunday after the first full moon following the vernal equinox, has also made it an occasion for the celebration of spring and the renewal of life.

The cultural significance of Easter

Easter is a significant cultural event, with a long history of art, music, literature, and traditions associated with it. Many famous works of art, such as Leonardo da Vinci's "The Last Supper" and Michelangelo's "Pieta," depict scenes from the Easter story. Easter hymns and music, such as Handel's "Messiah" and Bach's "St. Matthew Passion," are still performed and enjoyed today. Easter traditions such as the Easter egg hunt and the Easter parade have become a part of popular culture in many countries.

In conclusion, Easter is a significant celebration with both religious and cultural significance. Whether celebrated for its spiritual meaning, secular traditions, or cultural heritage, Easter remains an important time for reflection, renewal, and the celebration of life.

Easter Beyond the Religious Context:

Easter is a religious holiday that commemorates the resurrection of Jesus Christ. However, it has also become a cultural event that is celebrated by many people who do not necessarily observe the religious significance of the holiday. In this article, we will explore the non-religious ways that people celebrate Easter.

The Secular Celebration of Easter

Easter has become a time of celebration, regardless of religious affiliation. It is a time when families come together to enjoy each other's company, eat good food, and have fun. Many people take advantage of the long weekend and use it as an opportunity to travel, visit friends and family, or engage in outdoor activities.

One of the most popular secular traditions associated with Easter is the Easter egg hunt. Children hunt for Easter eggs that are hidden in the yard or house, and the person who finds the most eggs is declared the winner. The eggs are usually filled with candy, and some are even decorated with colourful designs or pictures.

Another popular secular Easter tradition is the Easter basket. Parents often fill baskets with candy and small toys, and hide them around the house for their children to find. The Easter bunny is also a secular symbol of the holiday, with many children eagerly awaiting the arrival of the bunny who is believed to bring Easter eggs and candy.

The Commercialization of Easter

As with many holidays, Easter has also become commercialized. Retailers take advantage of the holiday to sell Easter-related merchandise, such as chocolates, stuffed animals, and Easter decorations. In recent years, there has been a growing trend of "Easter gifts" being given to loved ones, similar to the tradition of giving Christmas gifts.

While some argue that the commercialization of Easter detracts from its religious significance, others see it as a natural evolution of the holiday, reflecting the changing cultural values and practices.

Non-Religious Ways to Celebrate Easter

For those who do not celebrate Easter in a religious context, there are still many ways to observe the holiday. Some people choose to volunteer at a local shelter or food bank, giving back to their community in the spirit of the holiday. Others take advantage of the long weekend to engage in outdoor activities, such as camping or hiking.

Many non-religious families have also created their own traditions associated with Easter. For example, some families choose to have a big Easter brunch, while others have a picnic in the park. Some families even have their own non-religious Easter egg hunts, using plastic eggs filled with toys and small gifts.

In conclusion, while Easter is a religious holiday, it has also become a cultural event that is celebrated by people of all faiths and backgrounds. Whether it is through the Easter egg hunt, the Easter basket, or the Easter bunny, the holiday provides an opportunity for families to come together, have fun, and create their own traditions.

Conclusion

The story of Easter is one of the most important stories in Christianity, but its relevance goes beyond the religious context. It speaks to the human experience in a way that is both timeless and universal. The themes of sacrifice, love, and redemption are as relevant today as they were thousands of years ago.

In a world that is often marked by pain, suffering, and injustice, the story of Easter provides hope and comfort. It reminds us that even in the darkest moments, there is the possibility of renewal and rebirth. The message of Easter is one of love, forgiveness, and second chances. It encourages us to extend grace to ourselves and to others, and to never give up on the possibility of a better tomorrow.

The Easter story is also relevant in our cultural lives. It has inspired countless works of art, music, and literature, and has become a beloved holiday that is celebrated around the world. Easter eggs, bunnies, and other symbols have become a part of our popular culture, and the message of hope and renewal that they represent is something that resonates with people of all ages and backgrounds.

Ultimately, the ongoing relevance of the Easter story is a testament to its power and its enduring significance. Whether you are a devout Christian or simply someone who appreciates the beauty and depth of the human experience, the story of Easter is one that will continue to inspire and touch our hearts for generations to come.

Frequently Asked Questions.

What is Easter Monday ?

Easter Monday is a holiday that is celebrated the day after Easter Sunday. It is a Christian holiday that celebrates the resurrection of Jesus Christ. Easter Monday is a public holiday in many countries, including Australia, Canada, the United Kingdom, and the United States. Easter Monday is the second day of the Easter long weekend. It is a day off work for many people, and a day for family and friends to get together. For Christians, it is a day to celebrate the resurrection of Jesus Christ. Christians believe that Jesus Christ was crucified on Good Friday and rose from the dead on Easter Sunday. Easter Monday is the day after Jesus Christ's resurrection. It is a day to celebrate new life and hope. Easter Monday is also known as Renewal Monday. It is a day to reflect on the events of Easter weekend and to renew our faith. In some countries, Easter Monday is a day of service. Churches may hold special services or Easter Egg hunts. In other countries, it is a day for relaxation and fun. Many people spend Easter Monday at the beach or in the park. Easter Monday is a public holiday in many countries. This means that schools and businesses are closed. Public transport may also be disrupted. If you are celebrating Easter Monday, we hope you have a happy and safe holiday!

What is Easter and why do we celebrate it?

Easter is one of the most important holidays in the Christian calendar, and celebrates the resurrection of Jesus Christ. The word Easter comes from the Old English word 'eastre', which is believed to be of Germanic origin. It is a time of renewal, and marks the end of the Lenten period of fasting and abstinence. Easter is a time to come together as a family and celebrate new life. It is a time of hope and thanksgiving. For many, it is also a time to reflect on the sacrifice that Jesus made for us. Easter is a special time to remember that we are never alone, and that no matter what happens in this life, God is always with us.

How is Easter celebrated in ?

Easter is one of the most important holidays in the Christian calendar, and its celebration has evolved over the centuries. In most Western countries, Easter is celebrated on the first Sunday following the full moon after the vernal equinox. This date can fall anywhere between March 22 and April 25. The holiday commemorates the resurrection of Jesus Christ, which is said to have occurred on the third day after his crucifixion. The word "Easter" is thought to come from the Old English "Ēastre" or "Ēostre", the name of an Anglo-Saxon goddess of spring and fertility. Easter Sunday is typically a day of church services and family gatherings. In many Christian homes, the Easter bunny is said to lay eggs overnight, which are then found by children in the morning. Chocolate eggs and bunnies are popular Easter gifts, and many families also enjoy a traditional Easter feast. In some parts of the world, such as the Philippines, Easter is celebrated with a more somber tone. Good Friday is observed as a day of fasting and prayer, and many people attend church services on Easter Sunday.

Why is Easter all about Jesus?

Easter is a religious holiday that celebrates the resurrection of Jesus Christ. Christians believe that Jesus died on the cross to save humanity from their sins, and that he rose from the dead three days later. Easter is considered to be the most important holiday in the Christian calendar, as it commemorates the most important event in Christian belief. Most Christians believe that Jesus was born of a Virgin Mother, and that he was without sin. They also believe that he died on the cross to save humanity from their sins. Jesus is seen as the ultimate example of love and sacrifice, and his resurrection is seen as a symbol of hope and new life. Easter is a time for Christians to come together to celebrate their faith, and to remember the ultimate sacrifice that Jesus made for them.

Do Maori celebrate Easter?

Do Maori celebrate Easter? Easter is a religious holiday that commemorates the resurrection of Jesus Christ. It is observed by Christians around the world and is typically a time for family gatherings and special meals. For many, it is also a time for exchanging gifts and enjoying fun activities like egg hunts. So, do Maori celebrate Easter? The answer is yes, but perhaps not in quite the same way as other Christians. While the holiday is celebrated by some Maori Christians, it is not as widely observed as it is in other parts of the world. This is likely due to the fact that the Maori population is only about 1 percent of the total population of New Zealand. Still, those who do celebrate Easter typically do so with traditional Maori ceremonies and celebrations. One such tradition is the lighting of a special bonfire on Easter Sunday. This represents the coming of spring and the new life that is associated with the holiday. Other common activities include feasts, singing, and the sharing of gifts. Overall, Easter is not as widely celebrated by Maori as it is by other Christians. However, those who do choose to celebrate the holiday do so in a uniquely Maori way.

Why do we celebrate Good Friday?

It is widely understood that Good Friday commemorates the day of Jesus Christ's crucifixion. However, there is more to the holiday than that. Good Friday is also a reminder of Jesus's resurrection and our own eventual resurrected life after death. Below are three reasons why Good Friday is such an important day of remembrance. First, Good Friday is a reminder of God's immense love for us. The day Jesus was crucified was one of great suffering, but it was also a day of great love. Jesus gave up his life so that we might have eternal life. As the Bible says, "For God so loved the world that he gave his one and only Son, that whoever believes in him shall not perish but have eternal life" (John 3:16). This is the ultimate demonstration of love, and it is a love that we are called to imitate. Second, Good Friday is a reminder of Jesus's victory over death. Jesus's death on the cross might have seemed like a defeat, but it was actually a great victory. Jesus conquered death so that we might have life. As the Bible says, "Death has been swallowed up in victory" (1 Corinthians 15:54). This is a victory that we can celebrate because it means that death is not the end. Third, Good Friday is a reminder of our own future resurrection. Because Jesus conquered death, we know that we, too, will one day be raised from the dead. As the Bible says, "We will be with the Lord forever" (1 Thessalonians 4:17). This is a hope that we can cling to in the midst of suffering, because we know that there is something better waiting for us. Good Friday is a day of great significance. It is a day that reminds us of God's love for us, of Jesus's victory over death, and of our own future resurrection. As we commemorate Good Friday, let us remember that because of what happened on that day, we have hope in the midst of suffering.

What does the Easter Bunny have to do with Jesus?

The Easter Bunny is a popular figure associated with Easter, but where did this bunny come from and what does it have to do with Jesus? The origins of the Easter Bunny are a bit of a mystery. Some say that the Easter Bunny was originally a symbol of the pagan goddess Eostre, from whom the holiday gets its name. Eostre was the goddess of spring and fertility, and her symbols were the hare and the egg. The egg, in particular, was thought to be a symbol of new life and rebirth. The Easter Bunny first appeared in German folk tales in the 1600s. According to one story, a poor old woman had no children to help her around the house. One Easter, she found a nest of eggs in her garden and decided to care for them as if they were her own. When they hatched, out came a bunny who then helped the woman with her chores. The Easter Bunny eventually made its way to America, where it became a popular symbol of Easter. And while the Easter Bunny may not have anything directly to do with Jesus, the holiday of Easter is a Christian celebration of Jesus' resurrection from the dead. So in a way, the Easter Bunny does have something to do with Jesus!

Easter is a time to come together and celebrate. It's a time for family, friends, and loved ones. It's a time to reflect on the past year and look forward to the year ahead. It's a time to be thankful for what we have and to hope for what we might become. Easter is a time of hope and renewal, and we can all use a little bit of that right now.

Why is it called Good Friday?

There are a few different theories about the origins of the term "Good Friday." One idea is that it comes from the expression "God's Friday," which was used by the Anglo-Saxons. Another possibility is that it was derived from the German word for Friday, "Friedag." In old English, the term "good" could mean either holy or happy. So why is the day called Good Friday? One theory is that it is a reference to the day of Christ's crucifixion being a "good" thing because it brought about forgiveness and redemption for humanity. According to Christians, through Christ's death and resurrection, they have the hope of eternal life. As the saying goes, "No cross, no crown." Good Friday is also considered good because it is a day of repentance and fasting. It is a day to reflect on Jesus' suffering and death and to remember that because of His great love for us, He was willing to go through all of that. Another explanation for the name is that it was simply a pleasant way to refer to the day without having to mention the Crucifixion, which was a very somber event. This theory is supported by the fact that the days leading up to Good Friday were originally referred to as "Holy Week," and the day after Good Friday was originally called "Easter Sunday." The term "Good Friday" is first found in print in the year 1563. It is used in a book called The whole Passion of Christ, compiled by a man named Percival Golding. Golding was not a clergyman, so some people believe that he might have been the one to come up with the name. Whatever the origins of the name, "Good Friday" is now a widely used term, and it serves as a reminder of the sacrificial love of Jesus Christ.

Why do they call it Easter?

There are many theories about the origins of the word "Easter", but no one knows for certain. One popular theory is that the word comes from "Eostre", the name of a pagan goddess of spring and fertility. According to this theory, pagans worshipped Eostre and held feasts and celebrations in her honor during the springtime. When Christianity began to spread throughout Europe, Christian missionaries tried to convert the pagans to their new religion. In order to make Christianity more appealing to the pagans, the missionaries kept some of the traditions and symbols of the pagan feast days, but gave them new Christian meanings. For example, the egg, which was a symbol of fertility for the pagans, became a symbol of Jesus' resurrection for Christians. Another theory about the origins of the word "Easter" is that it comes from the Old English word "eoster", which means "spring". This theory is supported by the fact that many other languages have similar words for "Easter" that are derived from words meaning "spring". For example, in French, the word for Easter is "Pâques", which comes from the Latin word "pascha", which means "Passover". In Spanish, the word for Easter is "Pascua", which comes from the same Latin root as the French word. So why do we call the holiday "Easter"? It's likely that the word has its origins in both pagan and Christian traditions. Whatever its origins, the word "Easter" has come to be associated with the most important holiday in the Christian calendar.

Can you drink on Easter Sunday?

The answer may seem simple - Easter is a religious holiday, so of course you can't drink! However, many people do choose to drink on Easter Sunday, and there are a few different reasons why. For some, Easter is a time to relax and celebrate with family and friends, and what better way to do that than with a lovely glass of wine or a refreshing beer? If you're going to be spending time with loved ones, you may as well enjoy a drink or two. others see Easter as a time for reflection and contemplation. Drinking alcohol can help to ease the mind and allow you to reflect on the Meaning of Easter. It can also be a way to connect with others, as sharing a drink is often seen as a sign of friendship and camaraderie. And of course, there are those who simply see Easter as an excuse to party! If you're looking to let loose and have a good time, then there's nothing wrong with enjoying a few drinks. So, can you drink on Easter Sunday? The answer is yes - but it's up to you to decide whether or not it's appropriate for the occasion. If you do choose to drink, be sure to drink responsibly and enjoy the holiday!

Why can't you buy alcohol on Easter Sunday?

Easter Sunday is a religious holiday for Christians that commemorates the resurrection of Jesus Christ. Because of the religious significance of the holiday, many Christians abstain from drinking alcohol on Easter Sunday. There are a number of reasons why Christians might choose not to drink alcohol on Easter Sunday. For some, the holiday is a time of reflection and spiritual contemplation, and abstaining from alcohol helps to create a more focused and reverent atmosphere. For others, Easter Sunday is a day of celebration and joy, and they believe that abstaining from alcohol helps to create a more wholesome and family-friendly atmosphere. Still others may choose not to drink alcohol on Easter Sunday as a way of showing respect for the religious beliefs of others. Whatever the reason, Christians who choose not to drink alcohol on Easter Sunday are certainly not alone. In fact, many Christians throughout the world abstain from drinking alcohol on this day.

What are 3 Easter traditions?

Easter traditions vary from family to family, but there are a few that are enjoyed by many. One tradition is hiding Easter eggs for the kids to find. This can be done inside the house or outside in the yard. Another popular tradition is making an Easter basket filled with goodies for the kids. And of course, no Easter would be complete without a delicious Easter dinner. For many families, the Easter holiday is a time to get together and celebrate. Easter dinner is often a time for family and friends to gather around the table and enjoy a meal together. A traditional Easter dinner may include ham, roasted potatoes, green beans, and rolls. Of course, no Easter dinner is complete without a dessert. A popular Easter dessert is the Easter bunny cake, which is a chocolate cake with white frosting and candy eggs on top. Easter is a time to celebrate the resurrection of Christ and the beginning of spring. It is a time to come together as a family and to enjoy each other's company. These are just a few of the many traditions that families enjoy during this Easter season.

Why do we hide eggs on Easter?

Easter eggs are a popular tradition associated with the holiday of Easter. The eggs are typically hidden for children to find, and the tradition is said to have originated with the Christian holiday of Easter. The egg is a symbol of spring and new life, and the act of hiding them is said to represent the act of God hiding the crucifixion from the eyes of the world. The tradition of hiding eggs is said to have started with the early Christians in Mesopotamia. They would hide eggs in gardens and bushes for children to find. The tradition eventually spread to Europe, where the eggs were often hidden in straw baskets or on clotheslines. In Germany, the tradition of hiding eggs in baskets eventually developed into the Easter Bunny, a popular figure associated with the holiday. The eggs are often hidden in difficult to find places, such as under furniture or in drawers. The challenge of finding the eggs is part of the fun, and children often work together in teams to find them all. Once all the eggs have been found, they are often gathered up and taken home to be eaten or used in other holiday recipes. The tradition of hiding eggs on Easter is a fun and festive way to celebrate the holiday. It is a popular tradition among Christians and non-Christians alike, and is a great way to bring family and friends together.

Why is Easter celebrated with a bunny?

Easter is a religious holiday that commemorates the resurrection of Jesus Christ. Christians believe that Jesus rose from the dead on the third day after his crucifixion, and Easter celebrates this event. The holiday is also celebrated with symbols such as eggs and rabbits, which represent new life. Rabbits are a symbol of fertility, and their association with Easter may date back to pagan traditions. Eggs are also a symbol of new life, and in many cultures, they are associated with spring. Christians believe that Jesus is the source of new life, and so eggs and rabbits came to be associated with Easter as symbols of his resurrection. Easter is a time for Christians to come together and celebrate new life. The holiday is also a time to reflect on Jesus Christ's sacrifice and what it means for Christians. The bunny and the egg are just two symbols that help to remind us of the true meaning of Easter.

When it comes to Easter, there are many different traditions that people follow. Whether it is dyeing eggs, going on an Easter egg hunt, or attending church, Easter is a time to celebrate the resurrection of Jesus Christ. For many, Easter is also a time to reflect on their own personal faith. No matter what your tradition is, Easter is a time to come together and celebrate.

Why do we have bunny and egg for Easter?

It's a common question every Easter - why do we have a bunny rabbit and eggs as symbols of the holiday? The answer actually has two parts. The first has to do with the origins of the holiday itself. Easter is a Christian holiday that celebrates the resurrection of Jesus Christ. It falls on the first Sunday after the first full moon following the spring equinox, making it a movable holiday (unlike Christmas, which always falls on December 25th). The word "Easter" is thought to come from the Anglo-Saxon goddess Eastre, who was associated with the Spring season. Her symbol was a bunny rabbit, which is likely how the Easter Bunny came to be. The second part of the answer has to do with the tradition of giving eggs for Easter. This is likely a carry-over from pagan tradition, as eggs have long been a symbol of new life and rebirth. In many ancient cultures, the egg was seen as a very powerful symbol, and was often associated with the sun. For early Christians, the egg became a symbol of the resurrection of Christ. So there you have it - the Easter Bunny and eggs are symbols of the holiday because they represent the origins of the holiday and the tradition of giving eggs as a symbol of new life.

Why does Easter change every year?

Easter is a religious holiday that celebrates the resurrection of Jesus Christ. Christians believe that Jesus rose from the dead after being crucified and that his resurrection offers salvation to all who believe in him. Easter falls on the first Sunday following the full moon after the vernal equinox, which means it can occur anywhere from March 22 to April 25. The earliest recorded observance of an Easter festival comes from the second century, though the holiday did not become formalized until the fourth century. Easter was originally a pagan holiday that celebrated the vernal equinox, which is the start of spring. The holiday was eventually Christianized, and the resurrection of Jesus became its central focus. While the religious aspects of Easter remain the same, the holiday has evolved over time. The most notable change is the date on which it is celebrated. This is because the Easter holiday is determined by the lunar cycle, and the date of the holiday moves around depending on when the full moon occurs. Some Christians believe that the date of Easter should always be the first Sunday after the first full moon of spring, regardless of the lunar cycle. Others believe that the holiday should be celebrated on the first Sunday after the vernal equinox. As a result, there is no one definitive date for Easter, and the holiday is celebrated on different dates by different Christian denominations. The date of Easter also affects how the holiday is celebrated. Many traditional Easter activities, such as dyeing eggs and eating chocolate, are tied to the vernal equinox and the start of spring. As a result, Easter celebrations often look different depending on when the holiday falls. Despite the changes that Easter has undergone over time, the holiday remains an important part of the Christian faith. For many Christians, Easter is a time to remember the sacrifice that Jesus made for their salvation. It is also a time to celebrate new life, both in Jesus and in the coming of spring.

Why do we not wish Good Friday?

Most Christians celebrate Good Friday as the day that Jesus Christ was crucified. It is a somber occasion, commemorated with prayer, fasting, and special services. For some, it is a day of sadness and reflection. For others, it is a day of thanksgiving, for the sacrifice that Jesus made for our sins. Why, then, do we not wish each other a "Happy Good Friday"? It may seem like a strange thing to say, but Good Friday is not a happy day. It is a day of mourning, of remembrance, and of reflection. On this day, we remember the suffering and the sacrifice of Jesus Christ. We reflect on his death, and on what it means for us and for our salvation. We do not wish each other a "Happy Good Friday" because it would be disingenuous. This is not a day for happiness, but for sadness and reflection. Good Friday is a day to remember the sacrifice of Jesus Christ, and to give thanks for his gift of salvation.

Can you wash on Good Friday?

There are many spiritual traditions surrounding the Easter holiday. For some, Good Friday is a day of mourning and reflection, while others may see it as a day of joy and celebration. But can you wash on Good Friday? The act of washing is often seen as a symbol of purification. In many religions, water is seen as a powerful cleansing agent that can wash away sin and impurities. For Christians, water is also seen as a symbol of new life and rebirth. baptism is one of the most important rituals in Christianity, and it involves washing in water. So, can you wash on Good Friday? There is no definitive answer. Some people believe that it is wrong to wash on Good Friday because it is a day of mourning and reflection. Others believe that it is perfectly fine to wash on Good Friday, as it is a day of new beginnings. Water is a powerful symbol, and how you choose to interpret its meaning is up to you.

Why is it called Good Friday when Jesus died?

There are a lot of myths and legends surrounding the origin of the term Good Friday. Some say that it is based on the term Good Friday because Jesus was crucified on a Friday. However, there is no evidence to support this claim. Others say that the term Good Friday is a Christian adaptation of the pagan holiday of Easter. Easter was a spring festival that celebrated the goddess Eastre. The Christians appropriated the holiday and renamed it Good Friday to commemorate the day of the crucifixion. Even though the exact origins of the term are unknown, we can be certain that it has become a day of religious significance for Christians around the world.

At what age does a child stop believing in the Easter Bunny?

When it comes to Easter, most children are probably all too familiar with the Easter Bunny. This furry rabbit is said to hop around hiding eggs and leaving them for children to find on Easter morning. Many children believe in the Easter Bunny wholeheartedly and are always excited to see what he has left for them come Easter. But at what point does a child stop believing in the Easter Bunny? It's hard to say for sure, but there are a few clues that suggest when a child might start to question the Easter Bunny's existence. For one, as children get older they begin to understand that bunnies don't lay eggs. When they realize that the Easter Bunny is supposedly doing something that bunnies can't do, they might start to question his existence. Another clue that a child might start to question the Easter Bunny's existence is if they never actually see the Easter Bunny themselves. If they've never seen him hiding eggs or delivering them on Easter morning, they might start to wonder if he's really just a made up character. So, while there's no definitive answer as to when a child stops believing in the Easter Bunny, there are a few key clues that suggest when a child might start to question his existence. And, in the end, whether or not a child believes in the Easter Bunny is totally up to them.

Why do you have chocolate eggs at Easter?

Why do you have chocolate eggs at Easter? One of the most popular food items associated with the Easter holiday is the chocolate egg. But why chocolate eggs? What is the significance of this tasty treat, and how did it become such a key part of Easter celebrations? The tradition of giving eggs at Easter is thought to date back to the 13th century, when eggs were given as gifts to mark the start of spring. The custom then spread to other parts of Europe, and by the 16th century, it was common for sugar-coated eggs to be given to children at Easter. It is thought that the first chocolate eggs were made in France in the early 19th century. These early chocolate eggs were quite different from the ones we eat today, being made of solid chocolate and often quite small. It wasn't until the late 19th century that chocolate eggs as we know them began to be made, with a hollow shell and a variety of different fillings. So, how did chocolate eggs become such a key part of Easter celebrations? It is thought that this is due to the influence of America. In the early 20th century, Easter eggs filled with candy were a popular treat in the US, and it is thought that this is where the idea of filling chocolate eggs with sweets originated. The first chocolate Easter eggs filled with candy were produced in Germany in the 1920s, and the tradition soon spread to other parts of Europe. These days, chocolate eggs are a staple of Easter celebrations all over the world. Whether they are filled with sweets or not, chocolate eggs are a delicious treat that has become firmly associated with this special time of year.

Easter is a time for family, friends, and celebrating the resurrection of Jesus Christ. It is a time of hope and love. Take the time to enjoy the company of those you love, and reflect on the meaning of Easter.

What is celebrated on Easter Monday?

Easter Monday is the second day of the Easter weekend and is typically celebrated with family and friends. For many, the day is spent attending church services, enjoying a large Easter feast, and spending time outdoors. Easter Monday is also a day where many people exchange Easter gifts, such as chocolate eggs and bunnies.

Is Easter Monday an official holiday?

Is Easter Monday an official holiday? Easter Monday is not an official holiday in the United States. However, many employers give their employees the day off work. In some states, schools are also closed on Easter Monday.

What happens on Holy Monday?

On Holy Monday, Christians remember the events that happened after Jesus Christ's crucifixion on Good Friday. Christ's body was taken down from the cross and buried in a tomb. On the third day, Easter Sunday, Christ rose from the dead and appeared to his disciples. The gospels of Matthew, Mark, and Luke all describe how, on the Sunday after the crucifixion, Mary Magdalene and other women went to the tomb where Christ had been buried and found that the stone had been rolled away and the tomb was empty. They then saw a man who they believed to be an angel, and he told them that Christ had risen from the dead. The gospels of John and Mark both describe how Christ appeared to Mary Magdalene after he had risen from the dead. John's gospel also describes how Christ appeared to two disciples on the road to Emmaus. On Easter Sunday, Christians celebrate Christ's resurrection. They believe that through Christ's death and resurrection, they have been forgiven and have the hope of eternal life.

Why do we celebrate Easter on Sunday instead of Monday?

EasterSunday is the most important day of the Christian year. It is the day when Christians celebrate the resurrection of Jesus Christ. Christians believe that Jesus is the Son of God who was sent to Earth to save humanity from sin. They believe that he died on the cross to save them from their sins and that he was resurrected on the third day. The resurrection of Jesus is the most important event in Christianity because it shows that Jesus has the power to defeat death. This event provides hope for Christians that they will also be resurrected after they die. Easter is celebrated on Sunday because it is the day of the week when Jesus was resurrected. Christians believe that Jesus rose from the dead early on Sunday morning. Some people think that we should celebrate Easter on Monday because it is the day of the week when Jesus appeared to his disciples after his resurrection. However, the most important day of the Christian year is Sunday because it is the day when we celebrate the resurrection of Jesus Christ.

What is the difference between Easter and Easter Monday?

The Difference between Easter and Easter Monday Easter is a religious holiday that celebrates the resurrection of Jesus Christ. It is observed by Christians throughout the world and is considered one of the most important holidays in the Christian faith. Easter Monday is not a religious holiday but is a day of celebration in many countries. It is a public holiday in many countries and is often used as a day for family gatherings and celebrations.

Is Easter Monday a holy day for Catholic Church?

Yes, Easter Monday is a holy day for the Catholic Church. In the Catholic tradition, Easter Monday is the second day of the Easter octave, which is eight days of celebrations commemorating the Resurrection of Jesus Christ. The first day of the octave is Easter Sunday, and the last day is Divine Mercy Sunday. Easter Monday has a special mass and readings associated with it, and many Catholics attend church on this day to celebrate the Resurrection of Christ. Many Catholics also observe Lenten traditions on Easter Monday, such as eating fish or abstaining from meat. Like all holy days of obligation, Catholics are expected to attend mass on Easter Monday. However, since it falls on a Monday, many people have to work and may not be able to attend. In these cases, Catholics are still obligated to attend mass at some point during the Easter octave. Overall, Easter Monday is a special day for Catholics to celebrate the Resurrection of Jesus Christ. While it is not a major holiday like Easter Sunday, it is still a day of rejoicing and celebration for many Catholics.

Do you get double pay on Good Friday?

The day on which Jesus Christ was crucified is known as Good Friday. The name is derived from the fact that Jesus died on the cross to save mankind from their sins. The day is considered to be a holy day by Christians, and many people take the day off from work to attend church services or other religious activities. Some employers offer their employees the option of taking the day off with pay, but not all companies do this. In general, Good Friday is considered to be a regular work day and employees are not given any special treatment. There is no federal law mandating that companies must give their employees paid time off for Good Friday, but some state laws do exist. For example, in New Jersey, employers are required to provide their employees with Good Friday as a paid holiday if the employee requests it. If you are wondering whether or not you will get paid double for working on Good Friday, the answer is most likely no. While some employers may offer their employees premium pay for working on a holiday, this is not required by law. Good Friday is not considered a federal holiday, so there is no legal obligation for companies to offer double pay. If you are considering taking the day off on Good Friday, you should check with your employer to see if they offer paid time off for the holiday. Some employers may be willing to give you the day off, but they are not required to do so.

Easter is a time of joy, hope, and new beginnings. It is a time to celebrate the resurrection of Jesus Christ and to remember that He is the hope of the world. Easter is a time to come together as family and friends and to rejoice in the good news of the gospel.

What happens on Easter Sunday?

Easter Sunday is the day when Christians celebrate the resurrection of Jesus Christ. It is the most important day of the Christian calendar, and is a time for families and friends to come together to celebrate. For many Christians, Easter Sunday is a day of worship and prayer. Some will attend special Easter services at their church, while others will spend time in prayer at home. Some Christians also choose to celebrate by going on an Easter egg hunt, or by eating special Easter food. Easter Sunday is a time to remember that Jesus died on the cross for our sins, and that he rose again three days later. It is a time to celebrate new life, and to remember that even in the darkest of times, hope is always with us.

What did Jesus do on a Monday?

Monday is the day that Jesus Christ rose from the dead, according to the Bible. This event is commemorated by Christians around the world with Easter celebrations. On the first Easter Monday, Jesus appeared to his disciples and showed them his wounds, proving that he had truly been resurrected. He then ascended into heaven, leaving them with the mission to spread the good news of salvation. For Christians, Easter Monday is a day of rejoicing and celebrating the most important event in their faith – the resurrection of Jesus Christ. It is a day to remember that through Christ's death and resurrection, they have been given the ultimate gift of life eternal.

What does the Bible say happened Easter Monday?

On Easter Monday, many Christians believe that Jesus Christ rose from the dead. The Bible does not specifically mention Easter Monday, but it does describe what happened on the Sunday following Jesus' crucifixion. According to the Bible, Jesus' disciples were gathered together in a room with the door locked, for they were afraid of the Jewish leaders. Suddenly, Jesus appeared in the room and said, "Peace be with you!" He then showed them His hands and side, providing proof that He had truly risen from the dead. Afterward, Jesus blessed them and said, "As the Father has sent me, I am sending you." These events occurred on a Sunday, but the Bible does not mention what happened on the following day, Easter Monday. Some biblical scholars believe that the disciples may have continued to meet together on that day, as they were instructed to do by Jesus. Others believe that they may have gone out into the community to share the news of Jesus' resurrection. Regardless of what the disciples did on Easter Monday, their lives were forever changed by the risen Savior. Today, many Christians celebrate Easter Monday as a day to remember Jesus' resurrection. Some churches hold special services, and many people use the day to spending time with family and friends. It is a day to rejoice in the knowledge that Jesus is alive and that we, too, can have eternal life.

What should we avoid during Holy Week?

As Christians, Holy Week is a time when we remember and reflect upon the events leading up to the crucifixion and resurrection of Jesus Christ. It is a time of solemnity and introspection, and as such, there are certain things that we should avoid during this week. Firstly, we should avoid any needless and meaningless distractions. This means turning off the television, putting down our phones, and spending time in prayer and reflection. Instead of indulging in idle chatter, we should take the time to listen to God and to what he is saying to us. Secondly, we should avoid any type of excessive drinking or partying. Holy Week is not a time for revelry, but for thoughtfulness and repentance. We should be focusing on our relationship with God, not on earthly pleasures. Thirdly, we should avoid violence. This week is a time of peace and love, and we should be acting accordingly. Whether it is physical violence or emotional violence, we should be seeking to promote peace and healing in our lives and in the world. Fourthly, we should avoid materialism. This week is a reminder that things of this world are fleeting and that our true treasure is in Heaven. We should be focused on our spiritual lives, not on earthly possessions. Lastly, we should avoid gossip and rumors. This week is about love and forgiveness, and spreading malicious rumors does not reflect that. Instead, we should be using our words to build others up, to edify and encourage. So, during this Holy Week, let us seek to avoid distractions, violence, materialism, and gossip. Instead, let us focus on God, on prayer, and on love.

Did Jesus rise on Easter Sunday or Monday?

Easter is one of the most important holidays in Christianity, celebrating the resurrection of Jesus Christ. Theholiday can fall on either Sunday or Monday, depending on the lunar calendar. But did Jesus actually rise on Easter Sunday, or was it Easter Monday? The answer may surprise you. According to the Bible, Jesus was crucified on a Friday and rose from the dead on Sunday morning. But there's no mention of which day Easter actually fell on. The holiday wasn't even called Easter back then. In fact, it wasn't until the second century that the day was called Easter and began to be celebrated as a major Christian holiday. So what happened? Well, the early Christians had a problem. The Jewish calendar is based on the lunar cycle, and theDate of Easter changes every year as a result. This caused a lot of confusion for Christians who wanted to celebrate the resurrection of Jesus on the same day every year. In order to solve this problem, the Council of Nicaea was held in AD 325. This council was a meeting of Christian leaders from all over the world, and they decided that Easter would be celebrated on the first Sunday after the first full moon of the spring equinox. This way, Easter would always fall on a Sunday (the day of the resurrection), and it would be the same date every year. So, did Jesus rise on Easter Sunday or Easter Monday? The answer is both. Because the holiday is based on the lunar calendar, the date of Easter can vary from year to year. But no matter when it falls, Easter always celebrates the resurrection of Jesus Christ and is a reminder of His sacrifice for our sins.

Which Easter is correct Catholic or Orthodox?

Easter is the most important holiday in Christianity, and it is celebrated in many different ways around the world. One of the most common questions about Easter is which tradition is the correct one – Catholic or Orthodox? There are actually many different types of Easter, as different Christian denominations celebrate the holiday in different ways. However, the two main traditions are Catholic and Orthodox. The Orthodox Easter is actually later than the Catholic Easter, as it is based on the old Julian calendar rather than the modern Gregorian calendar. This means that Orthodox Easter can be as much as five weeks after Catholic Easter. The main difference between the two traditions is that Orthodox Christians use unleavened bread for their communion, while Catholics use unleavened or unleavened wafers. Orthodox Christians also typically fast for 40 days before Easter, while Catholics do not have a set fasting period. Ultimately, there is no correct answer to which Easter tradition is the correct one. It is up to each individual to decide which tradition they want to follow.

What is Rule for Easter?

Rule for Easter is a Christian festival and holiday commemorating the resurrection of Jesus Christ on the third day after his crucifixion. Easter is considered the pinnacle of the Christian year by many Christians. It is the oldest and most important religious festival in the Western Christian calendar. The date of Easter varies from year to year. It falls on the Sunday between the dates of March 22 and April 25. Easter is always a moveable feast, which means it does not fall on a set date each year. The date of Easter is determined by the ecclesiastical approximation of the vernal equinox. There are many traditions and activities associated with Easter. Christians typically attend church services on Easter Sunday. They also exchange Easter eggs and give each other gifts. Easter is a time of renewal and hope for Christians.

Easter is a religious holiday that celebrates the resurrection of Jesus Christ. It is observed by Christians around the world and is a time for reflection, prayer, and spending time with family and friends. Easter is also a time for celebrating new life and the hope that spring brings.

What days over Easter can you not buy alcohol?

In some parts of the world, such as the United States, alcohol is not sold on Sundays. However, in other parts of the world, such as the United Kingdom, alcohol can be bought on any day of the week. So, what days over Easter can you not buy alcohol? In the United States, alcohol is not sold on Sundays. This means that if Easter falls on a Sunday, you will not be able to buy alcohol that day. In the United Kingdom, however, alcohol can be bought on any day of the week, including Easter Sunday. So, in summary, if you are in the United States, you will not be able to buy alcohol on Easter Sunday. However, if you are in the United Kingdom, you will be able to buy alcohol on Easter Sunday.

Can a Catholic drink on Good Friday?

Can a Catholic drink on Good Friday? It's a common question, and one that doesn't have a simple answer. Good Friday is the day on which Catholics commemorate the crucifixion of Jesus Christ. It is a day of fasting and abstinence, which means that Catholics are not supposed to eat or drink anything for the entire day. However, there are some exceptions to this rule. For example, pregnant women and young children are allowed to drink water and juice. And people who are sick are allowed to drink whatever they need to maintain their health. So, what about alcohol? Can Catholics drink on Good Friday? The answer is that it depends. Some Catholics choose to abstain from alcohol on Good Friday as a way of honoring the day. Others may not drink because they are already fasting and don't want to add anything else to their fast. Still, other Catholics may choose to drink on Good Friday as a way of celebrating the fact that Jesus died for our sins. After all, wine is a symbol of joy in the Catholic Church. Ultimately, the decision of whether or not to drink on Good Friday is up to each individual Catholic. There is no right or wrong answer, and each person must decide what is best for them.

Why do we celebrate Easter Sunday?

On Easter Sunday, Christians around the world celebrate the resurrection of Jesus Christ. This holiday has been celebrated for centuries, and its meaning has been passed down from generation to generation. Christians believe that Jesus is the son of God, and that he died on the cross to save humanity from their sins. His resurrection is seen as the ultimate act of love and sacrifice, and is a symbol of hope and new life. For many people, Easter is a time to reflect on their faith and to celebrate the hope that Christ brings. It is also a time to come together with family and friends, and to enjoy special meals and traditions. Whatever your reason for celebrating, Easter is a special time of year to remember the sacrifice of Jesus Christ and to celebrate his resurrection.

What Easter Sunday means?

On Easter Sunday, Christians celebrate the resurrection of Jesus Christ. This holiday has a deep meaning for Christians, as it is a reminder of Christ's sacrifice for humanity. The story of Easter begins with the Crucifixion of Jesus Christ. After Jesus was crucified, he was buried in a tomb. On the third day, he rose from the dead and appeared to his disciples. The resurrection of Jesus is a sign of hope for Christians. It is a reminder that after death, there is life. This event is also a reminder of God's power. The resurrection shows that nothing is impossible for God. For Christians, Easter is a time to reflect on the sacrifice of Jesus Christ and celebrate his victory over death. It is a time to come together as a community and celebrate the hope that Christ brings.

What happened on Easter Sunday?

On Easter Sunday, Christians around the world celebrate the resurrection of Jesus Christ. This holiday commemorates the day that Jesus rose from the dead after being crucified, an event that is central to Christian belief. For many Christians, Easter is a time of joy and celebration. It is a time to come together with family and friends, and to remember the sacrifice that Jesus made for all of humanity. It is also a time to reflect on the hope that comes with the belief in Jesus Christ, and the assurance of eternal life. For some, Easter may also be a time of contemplation and introspection. This holiday can be a reminder of the human capacity for evil and violence, and of the need for redemption and forgiveness. It can also be a time to reflect on the fragility of life, and the importance of cherishing every moment. No matter what Easter means to you, it is a day to remember the power of love, and the hope that springs eternal.

Why is Jesus important to Easter?

The resurrection of Jesus Christ is the central tenet of the Christian faith. Without it, Christianity simply wouldn't exist. But why is the resurrection so important? And what does it have to do with Easter? In short, the resurrection proves that Jesus is who He said He was, the Son of God. And if Jesus is the Son of God, then His death on the cross actually atoned for our sins, as He said it would. The resurrection also means that death is not the end. What a Hope-filled message that is! It means that if we put our trust in Jesus, we, too, will be resurrected to eternal life when He returns. So why is Jesus' resurrection important to Easter? Because without it, there would be no Easter. Easter is the day we celebrate Jesus' resurrection. On that first Easter Sunday, Jesus conquered death once and for all. And because He did, we can have hope that death is not the end for us, either. When we put our trust in Jesus and follow Him, we can have the assurance that we, too, will be resurrected to eternal life. That's something to celebrate!

What do people do on Easter?

What do people do on Easter? Most people in the United States celebrate Easter as a religious holiday. On Easter Sunday, people go to church and listen to a sermon about the resurrection of Jesus Christ. After church, many people have a big Easter dinner with their families. Some people also dye eggs and have an Easter egg hunt. Easter is a time for many people to reflect on their faith. For Christians, Easter is a reminder of the importance of Jesus Christ and his teachings. For people of other faiths, Easter can be a time to celebrate the start of spring. Easter is also a time to spend time with family and friends, and to enjoy the warmer weather after a long winter.

Easter is a holiday that is celebrated by Christians around the world. It commemorates the resurrection of Jesus Christ and is a time of joy and celebration. Easter is also a time for family and friends to get together and share in the joy of the season.

What happens to Jesus in Easter?

When most people think of Easter, they think of bunnies, eggs, and chocolate. But Easter is actually a religious holiday that celebrates the resurrection of Jesus Christ. So what exactly happens to Jesus in Easter? Well, according to the Bible, Jesus was crucified on Good Friday. He died and was buried in a tomb. But on Easter Sunday, he rose from the dead. This event is known as the Resurrection, and it is the central focus of Easter. For Christians, the Resurrection is a sign that Jesus is the Son of God, and that he has the power to forgive our sins. It is also a sign of hope; hope that we will one day be resurrected from the dead, and that we will have eternal life in heaven. So, this Easter, as you enjoy your chocolate eggs and bunnies, remember the true meaning of the holiday. And celebrate the hope that we have in Jesus Christ.

What are some fun facts about Easter?

What are some fun facts about Easter? Easter is a religious holiday that celebrates the resurrection of Jesus Christ. It is also a time for family and friends to get together and celebrate the beginning of spring. Easter eggs are a symbol of new life and are often decorate with symbols of spring. Easter bunny is also a popular symbol of Easter. It is said to bring Easter eggs to good children and deliver them on Easter morning. Easter traditions vary from country to country. In Germany, for example, children build Easter pyramids out of Easter baskets filled with candy and toys. In the Czech Republic, a popular Easter treat is mazurek, a pastry that is decorated with almonds, whipped cream, and chocolate. In Greece, Easter is celebrated with a traditional dish called magiritsa, which is a soup made with lamb offal. Easter is also a time for fun activities like Easter egg hunts and painting eggs.

How do you explain Easter to a child?

How do you explain Easter to a child? Easter is a religious holiday that celebrates the resurrection of Jesus Christ. It is observed by Christians all over the world and is one of the most important days in the Christian calendar. There are many ways to explain Easter to a child, but one of the most simple and effective ways is to talk about the Easter story. This is the story of how Jesus was crucified and died on the cross, but then he rose from the dead and conquered death. This story is at the heart of Easter, and it is a story that can inspire hope and joy in children. Another way to explain Easter to a child is to focus on the symbol of the Easter egg. This is a symbol of new life, and it can be a reminder that Easter is a time to celebrate new beginnings. eggs are often dyed or decorated, and they are often hidden for children to find. This can be a fun tradition for families to do together, and it can help to explain the meaning of Easter in a playful way. No matter how you choose to explain Easter to a child, the most important thing is to emphasize the meaning of hope and new life that Easter represents. This is a time of year when we can remember that death is not the end, and that there is always the potential for new beginnings.

What do do on Easter?

On Easter, many Christians celebrate Jesus Christ rising from the dead. In the Bible, Jesus died on the cross and was buried in a tomb. On the third day, he rose from the dead and appeared to his followers. Easter is a joyous occasion because it celebrates new life. Christians believe that Jesus is the Son of God and that his death and resurrection provide the way for humans to be forgiven and have eternal life. Because of this, Easter is a very important holiday for Christians. There are many different ways that Christians celebrate Easter. Some people attend special Easter services at church. Others spend time with family and friends. Some people give Easter baskets filled with goodies to loved ones. And of course, many people enjoy Easter egg hunts! Easter is a time to come together and celebrate new life. Whether you attend church, spend time with family and friends, or go on an Easter egg hunt, Easter is a time to rejoice!

What did Jesus do with Easter eggs?

Easter is a time to remember what Jesus did for us. He gave his life for our salvation. But what did he do with Easter eggs? Some people believe that Jesus may have used Easter eggs as a way to teach children about the resurrection. After all, an egg is a symbol of new life. When a chicken lays an egg, it is a reminder that something once small and insignificant can grow and thrive. Jesus may have also used Easter eggs to help people remember that he died on the cross. The egg's shell is hard and protects the fragile egg inside. In the same way, Jesus' body was strong enough to withstand the pain of the crucifixion so that we could be forgiven. No matter what the reason, Easter eggs are a fun and important part of Easter. They remind us of the hope that we have in Jesus Christ.

Why do we boil eggs on Easter?

There are many different traditions associated with Easter, but one of the most common is to boil eggs. But why do we do this? One theory is that the egg represents new life, and so boiling them is a way of symbolically cleansing them and starting afresh. This is particularly significant at Easter time, which is all about renewal. Another explanation is that boiling eggs was simply a way of preserving them for the Lenten period, when many people would not eat them. By boiling them, they would last longer and could be eaten after Lent had ended. Whatever the reason, boiling eggs has become a firm part of Easter tradition in many cultures, and is a fun activity to do with the whole family. So next time you're boiling eggs for Easter, take a moment to think about the history and symbolism behind this simple act.

Is Easter because of Jesus?

Easter is one of the most important holidays in Christianity, but there is some debate over its origins. Some scholars believe that Easter is a Christian adaptation of a pagan festival, while others believe that it is a purely Christian holiday. The word "Easter" is derived from the Old English word "Ēostre", which was the name of the Anglo-Saxon goddess of spring. Ēostre was associated with the Spring Equinox, and her festival was celebrated around the time of the Vernal Equinox. There were also pagan festivals that were celebrated around the time of the Spring Equinox, including the Roman festival of Cybele, which was a festival of fertility and rebirth. The early Christians were likely aware of these pagan festivals, and they may have adopted the name "Easter" and the date of the Spring Equinox for their own holiday. The first recorded celebration of Easter was in the year 336, when the Council of Nicaea set the date of Easter as the first Sunday after the first full moon after the Spring Equinox. The holiday of Easter has both pagan and Christian elements. The pagan elements are the Spring Equinox and the goddess Ēostre. The Christian elements are the resurrection of Jesus Christ and the celebration of his death and resurrection. Whether Easter is a purely Christian holiday or a Christian adaptation of a pagan festival, it is still an important holiday for Christians around the world.

Easter is a holiday that is celebrated by many people around the world. It is a time to come together and celebrate the resurrection of Jesus Christ. Easter is a time of hope and new beginnings. It is a time to reflect on the past and look forward to the future.

What special foods are eaten on Easter?

On Easter, many people enjoy special foods like ham, lamb, and Easter eggs. Easter ham is a traditional dish that many families enjoy on Easter Sunday. Ham is often served with green beans, potatoes, and a variety of other side dishes. Easter lamb is another popular dish that is often served on Easter. Lamb is a symbol of spring and new beginnings, and is often roasted and served with a variety of side dishes. Easter eggs are also a popular food on Easter. Easter eggs are often dyed and decorated, and are often hidden for children to find.

What is a fun question about Easter?

This Easter, instead of the usual egg hunt, why not try a hide-and-seek Easter bunny hunt? The Easter bunny can hide anywhere in the house or yard, and the kids have to find it. This is a great way to get everyone up and moving, and it can be a lot of fun for the whole family. Another fun Easter activity is an Easter egg decorating contest. Get some hard-boiled eggs and a bunch of different decorations, and let the kids go to town. They can use paints, stickers, glitter, or whatever they want to make their egg look the best. Then, have a vote to see which egg is the most creative. If you want to keep things really simple, you can always just have an Easter egg hunt. Hide some eggs around the house or yard, and let the kids go find them. You can make it a race to see who can find the most eggs, or you can just let everyone take their time and enjoy the hunt. Easter is a great time to get together with family and friends, and there are plenty of fun activities that you can do to celebrate. No matter what you end up doing, Easter is sure to be a blast.

What are main things in Easter?

Easter is a religious holiday that celebrates the resurrection of Jesus Christ. It is considered to be the most important holiday in the Christian faith. Christians believe that Jesus died on the cross and was resurrected three days later. This event is commemorated during Easter. The holiday of Easter is also celebrated with many secular traditions. Easter eggs and Easter bunnies are two of the most popular symbols of Easter. Easter eggs are often decorated and hidden for children to find. Easter bunnies are also popular symbols of the holiday. They are often portrayed as bringing Easter eggs to children. Easter is a time for family and friends to get together. Special meals and feasts are often prepared for this occasion. Easter is also a time for giving gifts, particularly to children. Easter is a very special holiday for Christians. It is a time to remember and celebrate the most important event in their faith. It is also a time to enjoy the company of family and friends and to partake in some of the many traditions that have developed over the years.

What is the most popular Easter activity?

One of the most popular Easter activities is attending church services. For many people, Easter is a religious holiday that commemorates the resurrection of Jesus Christ. Attending church is a way to remember and celebrate this event. Another popular activity is spending time with family and friends. This is often a time when people get together who don't see each other very often. It's a time to catch up and enjoy each other's company. Easter can be a very busy time for families, but it's also a time to relax and enjoy each other's company. Easter brunch is also a popular activity. This is often a time when family and friends get together to enjoy a nice meal. Easter brunch can be a very elaborate affair, or it can be a simple meal. Either way, it's a time to enjoy good food and good company. Some people also enjoy Easter egg hunts. This is a fun activity for both children and adults. Easter egg hunts can be a lot of fun, and they often result in a lot of laughter. Whatever you do this Easter, make sure to enjoy yourself. Easter is a time to celebrate, and to spend time with the people you care about.

How can I celebrate Easter Sunday at home?

Easter is a special time of year where family and friends get together to celebrate. There are many ways to celebrate Easter at home, whether it's going on an Easter egg hunt, decorating eggs, or having a special Easter meal. Here are some ideas to help make your Easter celebration at home special. An Easter egg hunt is a fun way to get everyone involved in the festivities. Hide plastic eggs around the house or yard and let the kids go on a hunt. If you want to make it more challenging, you could put a small prize in some of the eggs. Decorating eggs is another fun Easter activity. You can use food coloring to dye hard-boiled eggs, or get creative with other materials like paints, stickers, or glitter. Once they're decorated, you can put them on display or use them in an Easter egg hunt. If you're having a special Easter meal, you could make a bunny-shaped cake or cupcakes. Or, get creative with your Easter dinner and make Easter-themed foods like bunny-shaped sandwiches or deviled eggs. For dessert, you could make an Easter trifle or an Easter bunny cake. Whatever activities you choose to do, make sure to include some time for reflection and appreciation. Easter is a time to celebrate new beginnings, so take a moment to think about the things in your life that you're thankful for.

What do most families do on Easter?

What do most families do on Easter? Easter is a religious holiday that celebrates the resurrection of Jesus Christ. For many people, it is also a time to spend time with family, enjoy special meals and treats, and celebrate the beginning of spring. Most families have their own traditions for celebrating Easter. Some people attend church services on Easter Sunday, while others spend the day decorating eggs or going on Easter egg hunts. Some families also have a tradition of eating a special Easter meal together. No matter how you choose to spend Easter, it is a time to come together with loved ones and celebrate. So, what do most families do on Easter? They spend time together and create memories that will last a lifetime.

What is the basic story of Easter?

The Easter story is one of hope, new life, and redemption. The basic story goes like this: Jesus was a man who lived two thousand years ago in the Middle East. He was a teacher and miracle worker who had many followers. On the night before his execution, Jesus had a Last Supper with his disciples. He was betrayed by one of them, arrested, and put on trial. He was crucified by the Romans, and died. On the third day after his death, Jesus rose from the dead. He appeared to his followers and After appearing to his disciples, he ascended into heaven. Christians believe that because Jesus died and rose again, we can have hope for eternal life. Easter is a celebration of Jesus' resurrection, and a time to remember that hope.

Although the exact origins of Easter are unknown, the holiday has been celebrated for centuries. Easter is a time to come together and celebrate new beginnings. Whether you celebrate with a feast, an egg hunt, or simply by spending time with loved ones, Easter is a cherished tradition for many.

What is the story of Easter Bunny?

What is the story of Easter Bunny? The Easter Bunny is a popular figure associated with the holiday of Easter. According to legend, the Easter Bunny brings baskets of Easter eggs and candy to children on Easter morning. The Easter Bunny is said to be a symbol of new life and has been associated with the holiday since the 19th century. The origins of the Easter Bunny are disputed. Some say that the bunny was originally a pagan symbol of fertility and new life. Others believe that the tradition was started by German immigrants who brought the legend of an Easter Hare with them to the United States. Whatever the case may be, the Easter Bunny has become a cherished part of the Easter holiday for many people. Children enjoy hunting for Easter eggs and receiving candy from the Bunny. And for adults, the Easter Bunny can be a fun and festive way to celebrate the holiday.

What day was Jesus crucified on?

The crucifixion of Jesus is one of the most important events in history. Christians believe that Jesus was crucified on a Friday, which is why Good Friday is a holiday. Jews believe that Jesus was crucified on a Wednesday. There is some evidence to support both beliefs. The Gospels of Matthew, Mark, and Luke say that Jesus was crucified on the day after he was arrested, which would have been a Friday. The Gospel of John says that Jesus was crucified on the day before the Passover, which was a Thursday. Some people believe that Jesus was crucified on a Wednesday because that is the day that Judas Iscariot betrayed him. Judas Iscariot was one of Jesus' disciples. Judas Iscariot betrayed Jesus by kissing him on the cheek and telling the authorities where he was. The reason why there is confusion about the day of the crucifixion is because the Crucifixion was a Roman punishment, and the Romans did not keep track of the days of the week. The day of the crucifixion was not a holiday in the Roman Empire. Christians celebrate Good Friday because it is the day that Jesus died. Jesus died so that people could be forgiven for their sins. Christians believe that Jesus rose from the dead on Easter Sunday.

What are 8 facts about Easter?

What are 8 facts about Easter? 1. Easter is a religious holiday that celebrates the resurrection of Jesus Christ. 2. It is observed by Christians around the world and is considered one of the most important holidays in the Christian faith. 3. The date of Easter changes each year, but it is always celebrated on a Sunday in the spring. 4. In the Western Christian tradition, Easter is preceded by Lent, a 40-day period of fasting and prayer. 5. On Easter Sunday, Christians attend church services and celebrate with special meals and activities. 6. Common Easter symbols include eggs and rabbits, which represent new life and fertility. 7. Easter is also a time for giving and receiving gifts, and many people exchange Easter eggs filled with candy or other treats. 8. Easter is a popular time for vacations and travel, as many people take advantage of the long weekend to enjoy time with family and friends.

What is the moral of Easter?

The moral of Easter, like many popular religious holidays, is open to interpretation. To some, it is a time to celebrate the resurrection of Jesus Christ and the triumph of good over evil. To others, it is a time to reflect on the cycle of life, death, and rebirth. And still others see it as a time to come together with family and friends, and to cherish the time we have together. Whatever your interpretation may be, the moral of Easter is ultimately about hope. Hope for a better tomorrow, hope for a new beginning, and hope for a life eternal. It is a time to celebrate the fact that, despite the darkness and emptiness of death, life always finds a way to continue.

How do you explain the Easter Bunny to Jesus?

The Easter Bunny is a popular symbol of Easter that is used to represent the holiday in many ways. The most common image of the Easter Bunny is a white rabbit that is often depicted with colorful eggs, which are said to be left by the bunny for children to find on Easter morning. The Easter Bunny is also a popular motif on Easter cards and decorations. So how do you explain the Easter Bunny to Jesus? Well, it's actually quite simple. The Easter Bunny is a symbol of hope and new beginnings. Just as Jesus rose from the dead, so too does the Easter Bunny represent the hope of new life. The Easter Bunny also brings joy and happiness to children on Easter morning, just as Jesus brings hope and joy to all of us. So when you see the Easter Bunny this Easter, remember that he represents the hope and joy of Easter, and the new life that Jesus brings to us all.

What religion does not support Easter?

Easter is a religious holiday that celebrates the resurrection of Jesus Christ. Christians believe that Jesus was crucified and died on the cross, but was resurrected three days later. Easter is considered a very important holiday in the Christian faith, and is celebrated by millions of people around the world every year. There are a number of religions that do not support Easter. One of the most notable is Islam. Muslims believe that Jesus was a prophet, but they do not believe that he was resurrected. Therefore, they do not celebrate Easter. Other religions that do not support Easter include Buddhism, Hinduism, and Sikhism.

Can you serve alcohol on Easter Sunday ?

Easter is a time of year when many Christians celebrate the resurrection of Jesus Christ. It is also a time when family and friends get together to enjoy good food and company. For some, this may include serving alcohol. But can you serve alcohol on Easter Sunday? The answer may depend on where you live. In the United States, for example, federal law does not prohibit serving alcohol on Easter Sunday. However, individual states may have their own laws that do. So, it's always best to check with your local authorities before serving alcohol on Easter Sunday. While there may not be any legal restrictions on serving alcohol on Easter Sunday, some Christians may choose not to do so out of respect for the religious holiday. To them, Easter is a time to reflect on the resurrection of Jesus and not a time to drink. Others may argue that serving alcohol on Easter Sunday is perfectly fine. After all, the Bible does not explicitly forbid it. In fact, there are several instances where Jesus and his disciples drank wine. So, if it was good enough for Jesus, it's good enough for them! Regardless of what you believe, the decision to serve alcohol on Easter Sunday is a personal one. If you do choose to serve alcohol, be sure to do so responsibly. Offer non-alcoholic options for those who don't drink and make sure everyone gets home safe.

Easter is a Christian holiday that celebrates the resurrection of Jesus Christ. It is observed on the first Sunday after the first full moon following the vernal equinox. In the Western Christian tradition, Easter also marks the end of Lent, a 40-day period of fasting, prayer, and penance.

Is Easter a Catholic thing?

Easter is a religious holiday that celebrates the resurrection of Jesus Christ. It is observed by Christians all over the world and is considered one of the most important days in the Christian calendar. Many people believe that Easter is a Catholic holiday, but this is not strictly true. Easter is a Christian holiday, and as such, it is celebrated by all Christians, regardless of denomination. While the days and weeks leading up to Easter Sunday may vary slightly between Catholic and Protestant churches, the holiday itself is observed by both. The origin of Easter can be traced back to the early days of Christianity, and the holiday has been celebrated for over two thousand years. Easter is mentioned in the Bible, and it is thought to have arisen from pagan spring festivals. While Easter is celebrated by Christians of all denominations, it is particularly important to Catholics. For Catholics, Easter is the most important day of the year, and the Easter season is a time of great joy and celebration. Easter is a time to come together and celebrate our shared faith. Whether you are Catholic or Protestant, Christian or non-Christian, Easter is a holiday that is worth celebrating.

Is Easter Catholic or pagan?

Easter is one of the most important holidays in Christianity, celebrated as the day when Jesus Christ rose from the dead. However, there is some debate over whether Easter has paganroots. Easter falls at the end of Lent, a 40-day period of fasting and repentance. Lent originated as a way for Christians to prepare for Easter, but it also has roots in pagan spring festivals. Before Christianity became the dominant religion in the Roman Empire, people celebrated the arrival of spring with a festival called Lolth. Lolth was a goddess of fertility and new beginnings, and her festival was a time of feasting and merrymaking. As Christianity spread, the church adapted many pagan traditions to Christian holidays. For example, the Easter bunny and eggs are both symbols of fertility that were incorporated into the holiday. So, is Easter Catholic or pagan? The answer is both. Easter has both Christian and pagan roots, but it is primarily a Christian holiday.

What is the true meaning of Resurrection Sunday?

The death and resurrection of Jesus Christ is the central tenet of the Christian faith. In short, without the resurrection, Christianity would not exist. The apostles were eyewitnesses to the resurrection of Christ and therefore, their testimony is extremely important. The gospel accounts of the resurrection tell us that on the third day after Jesus died on the cross, He rose from the dead. This event changed everything. Not only did it prove that Jesus was who He said He was – the Son of God – but it also gave hope to all who would put their faith in Him. The resurrection proves that death is not the end. Christ conquered death and offers us the hope of eternal life. This hope is a result of the resurrection. Because Jesus was resurrected, we know that we, too, will be resurrected. The resurrection is also a victory over sin. When Jesus died on the cross, He took the punishment for our sin. But His resurrection shows that He has the power to overcome sin and death. The resurrection is a cause for hope and joy. It is a reminder that no matter what the world throws at us, we have the hope of eternal life with Christ. It is a reminder that nothing – not even death – can separate us from the love of God.

Why is it called Easter and not Resurrection Sunday?

There are a few different theories as to why the holiday of Easter is named after a pagan goddess instead of the Christian holiday of Resurrection Sunday. One theory is that the early Church wanted to Christianize the pagan festival of Ostara, and they did so by co-opting the name and traditions. Another theory is that the name Easter came about simply because it sounded similar to the word for "passover" in German. Whatever the reason for the name, it's clear that over time, the Christian holiday of Easter has come to be about much more than just the resurrection of Jesus Christ. For many people, Easter is a time to celebrate new beginnings, hope, and the joy of spring. It's a time to come together with family and friends, and to reflect on the important role that faith plays in our lives. No matter what we call it, Easter is a special time of year, and one that is worth celebrating.

Do Catholics celebrate Resurrection Sunday?

Catholics celebrate the resurrection of Jesus Christ every Easter Sunday. This holiday commemorates the day that Jesus rose from the dead after being crucified. Catholics believe that through Jesus' death and resurrection, we have been given the gift of eternal life. Easter is a very important holiday in the Catholic faith. It is a time of joy and celebration. Catholics believe that Jesus conquered death and that through him, we can have eternal life. Easter Sunday is a day of hope and new beginnings. Catholics prepare for Easter through a season of Lent. Lent is a time of prayer, reflection, and self-denial. It is a time to prepare our hearts and minds for Easter. On Easter Sunday, we celebrate the resurrection of Jesus Christ. We celebrate that through him, we have eternal life.

How do Christians celebrate Resurrection Sunday?

Resurrection Sunday, also known as Easter, is one of the most important days in the Christian calendar. It commemorates the day that Jesus Christ rose from the dead, and is celebrated by Christians all over the world. There are many different ways that Christians celebrate Easter, but some of the most common traditions include attending church services, giving gifts, and decorating eggs. Many Christians also choose to spend time with their families on this day, and enjoy special meals together. For many Christians, Easter is a time of joy and celebration. It is a time to remember the most important event in their faith, and to give thanks for the gift of eternal life.

What happens on Resurrection Day?

On Resurrection Day, Christians celebrating the holiday believe that Jesus Christ rose from the dead after being crucified. This event is said to have happened on the third day after his crucifixion. The day is marked by attending church services and participating in other religious activities. Many people also take the time to reflect on the meaning of the holiday and what it represents for them personally. For some, it is a time of joy and celebration, while for others it is a time of somber reflection and contemplation.

The Easter holiday is a time to celebrate the resurrection of Jesus Christ and to enjoy time with family and friends. For many, it is a time to reflect on their religious beliefs and to renew their faith. Easter is also a time for exchanging gifts, enjoying festive meals, and participating in fun activities like Easter egg hunts. No matter how you celebrate Easter, it is sure to be a special day.

What is the difference between Easter Sunday and Resurrection Sunday?

The Christian holiday of Easter celebrates the resurrection of Jesus Christ. It is considered the most important holiday in the Christian calendar. Resurrection Sunday is the day on which Christians celebrate the resurrection of Jesus Christ. It is the first Sunday after Good Friday, the day on which Jesus was crucified. Easter Sunday is the day on which Jesus rose from the dead, according to the Bible. The word "Easter" is derived from the Latin word for "spring," which is the season in which the holiday falls. Christians believe that Jesus was resurrected on the third day after his death on the cross. His resurrection proves that he is the Son of God, and it give hope to Christians that they, too, will be resurrected after death. The holiday of Easter is therefore a celebration of Jesus Christ's victory over death. Christians celebrate Easter with feasts, special church services, and the exchange of Easter eggs, which are symbolic of new life.

Why do Catholics call it Easter?

The most common understanding of the word "Easter" is that it refers to the Christian holiday celebrating the resurrection of Jesus Christ. However, the word "Easter" actually predates Christianity, and was originally a pagan holiday celebrating the Spring Equinox. So how did the word "Easter" come to be associated with the Christian holiday? One theory is that the word "Easter" comes from the name of the Germanic goddess Eastre. Eastre was associated with the Spring Equinox, and her feast day was celebrated on the vernal equinox. The Venerable Bede, an 8th-century English historian and monk, wrote that the Anglo-Saxon month of April was originally called "Eostremonath", named after Eastre. It's possible that the Christian holiday of Easter was originally named after the pagan goddess Eastre as a way of co-opting the holiday and converting pagans to Christianity. However, there is no definitive evidence that this is the case. Another theory is that the word "Easter" comes from the Hebrew word for Passover, "Pesach". This theory is supported by the fact that the timing of Easter coincides with the Jewish holiday of Passover. Whatever the origins of the word "Easter", it is now inextricably linked to the Christian holiday of the same name. Easter is a time of rebirth and hope, and is celebrated by Christians all over the world.

Is Easter ever mentioned in the Bible?

Easter is a special day for Christians, as it celebrates the resurrection of Jesus Christ. But is Easter ever mentioned in the Bible? Interestingly, the word 'Easter' is never mentioned in the Bible. However, there are a number of references to the resurrection of Jesus Christ, which took place on Easter Sunday. In the book of Matthew, we read about how Jesus was crucified and buried. On the third day, he rose from the dead and appeared to his disciples. This event is known as the resurrection, and it is the central message of Christianity. The resurrection is also mentioned in the book of Mark, Luke and John. In each of these books, we read about how Jesus died and was buried, and on the third day he rose from the dead. So, while the word 'Easter' is not mentioned in the Bible, the event that we celebrate on Easter Sunday – the resurrection of Jesus Christ – is mentioned numerous times. This event is the foundation of our faith, and it is what makes Easter such a special day.

Do Catholics believe in the resurrection of the dead?

The resurrection of the dead is one of the central beliefs of the Catholic faith. In the Apostles' Creed, we profess our belief in the "resurrection of the body". This means that, just as Jesus Christ was raised from the dead, we, too, will be raised from the dead. The Catechism of the Catholic Church teaches that "the resurrection of the dead is the final completion of the transformation of the human person into the likeness of Christ, according to the 'glorious bodies' of Genesis 1:26-27". In other words, at the resurrection, our bodies will be transformed into glorified bodies, like the body of Christ. The resurrection is a fundamental doctrine of the Catholic faith, and it is based on the risen Christ. When Jesus was crucified, he died a physical death. But on the third day, he rose from the dead, proving that he is both God and man. The resurrection of Christ is a historical fact that is attested to by eyewitnesses. The Gospels of Matthew, Mark, Luke, and John all record the events of Christ's resurrection. In addition, the early Christians were willing to die for their belief in the resurrection. The belief in the resurrection of the dead is also based on the teaching of Scripture. In the Old Testament, we see various references to the resurrection. For example, in the book of Isaiah, we read that the dead will be raised (Isaiah 26:19). In the book of Daniel, we read that the dead will be raised to everlasting life (Daniel 12:2). The New Testament is even more explicit in its teaching on the resurrection. In the Gospels, we see Jesus himself teaching on the resurrection (Matthew 22:29, Mark 12:24, Luke 20:37). In the book of Acts, we read about the early Christians sharing their faith in the resurrection (Acts 4:2, 17:18). And in the epistles, we see the apostles teaching on the resurrection (1 Corinthians 15:12-20, 1 Thessalonians 4:13-14). The resurrection of the dead is a central doctrine of the Catholic faith, and it is based on the risen Christ. When Jesus was crucified, he died a physical death. But on the third day, he rose from the dead, proving that he is both God and man. The resurrection of Christ is a historical fact that is attested to by eyewitnesses. The Gospels of Matthew, Mark, Luke, and John all record the events of Christ's resurrection. In addition, the early Christians were willing to die for their belief in the resurrection. The belief in the resurrection of the dead is also based on the teaching of Scripture. In the Old Testament, we see various references to the resurrection. For example, in the book of Isaiah

Why does Resurrection Sunday change every year?

As Christians, we celebrate the Resurrection of Jesus Christ every year on Resurrection Sunday, also known as Easter. But have you ever wondered why the date of Easter changes every year? The reason is actually quite simple. Easter is a moveable feast, which means that its date is not fixed in the calendar. The date of Easter is determined by the lunar cycle, and specifically, the date of the first full moon of Spring. In the Western Christian tradition, Easter always falls on the first Sunday after the first full moon of Spring. This can be anywhere from March 22 to April 25. In the Eastern Christian tradition, Easter is always celebrated on the first Sunday after the Paschal full moon, which is the first full moon of Spring according to the ecclesiastical rules. This can be anywhere from April 4 to May 8. So, why is Easter a moveable feast? The simple answer is that the date of Easter is based on the lunar cycle, which is different every year. The date of the first full moon of Spring can vary by a few days, which is why the date of Easter also changes. But there is also a deeper reason why Easter is a moveable feast. In the Bible, we read that the death and Resurrection of Jesus Christ occurred during the Jewish festival of Passover. The Jewish calendar is a lunar calendar, and so the festival of Passover occurs on the first full moon of Spring. So, in a sense, the date of Easter is a reminder that the death and Resurrection of Jesus Christ is the fulfillment of the Passover festival. When we celebrate Easter, we are celebrating the ultimate Passover, in which Jesus Christ was the perfect Lamb of God, sacrificed for our sins. Resurrection Sunday is a special day for Christians all over the world. It is a day when we remember and give thanks for the greatest act of love in history, the sacrificial death and glorious Resurrection of our Lord and Savior, Jesus Christ.

Is it right to say Happy Easter?

It's a common refrain around Easter time - is it really appropriate to say "Happy Easter"? After all, this holiday commemorates the crucifixion of Jesus Christ, one of the most solemn and significant events in Christian history. Surely a happy holiday can't be built on such a somber foundation, can it? Actually, there's a lot of support for the idea that Easter is, and should be, a happy occasion. First and foremost, Easter celebrates the resurrection of Jesus Christ, an event that Christians believe conquered death and ushered in eternal life. What could be happier than that? In addition, the resurrection story is just one example of the many instances in the Bible where good triumphs over evil, hope triumphs over despair. At a time when the world can seem dark and full of despair, a holiday that celebrates hope and joy is more important than ever. So go ahead and say "Happy Easter"! It's the perfect way to spread a little hope and happiness at a time when we all need it most.

Why is the resurrection day so important?

Easter is a day that Christians celebrate the resurrection of Jesus Christ. It is considered to be the most important day of the Christian year. The resurrection is significant because it shows that Jesus conquered death and that he is the Son of God. The resurrection also provides hope for Christians that they too will one day be resurrected. Easter is a time of joy and celebration for Christians as they remember the sacrifice that Jesus made for them and the hope that they have for eternal life.

While the origins of Easter are debated, the holiday has become a time for family, fun, and feasting. For Christians, Easter is a time to celebrate the resurrection of Jesus Christ. Whether you spend Easter with a religious ceremony or a day at the egg hunt, the holiday is a time to come together.

What is the color for Resurrection Sunday?

What is the color for Resurrection Sunday? For many people, the color of Resurrection Sunday is white. White is the color of purity and new beginnings, and it is often seen as the color of heaven. In the Christian faith, white is also the color of the resurrection of Jesus Christ. When Christ rose from the dead, he conquered sin and death, and brings new life to all who believe in him. For some people, the color of Resurrection Sunday is red. Red is the color of blood, and it is seen as the color of life. In the Christian faith, red is also the color of the love of Christ. Christ died on the cross for the forgiveness of our sins, and his love for us is shown in his willingness to sacrifice himself for us. No matter what color you choose to wear on Resurrection Sunday, the important thing is to remember what the day is all about. It is a day to celebrate the resurrection of Jesus Christ and to remember that because he lives, we can have hope for eternal life.

What is the importance of Resurrection Sunday?

The resurrection of Jesus Christ is the most important event in human history. On that first Easter Sunday, Jesus rose from the dead, proving once and for all that He is who He said He is—the Son of God and our Savior. Because He conquered death, we no longer need to fear death or the eternal consequences of our sin. We can have hope—hope for this life and hope for eternity. What does that hope mean for us today? Because Jesus is alive, we can be assured of His power to forgive our sin and to change our lives. When we put our faith in Him, He gives us a new life—a life that is empowered by the Holy Spirit to live for Him. He gives us the strength to overcome our sinful desires and to live according to His ways. Living for Jesus means following His commands and sharing His love with others. It means living in such a way that brings glory to God. It means living a life of sacrificial love, just as Jesus sacrificed His life for us. When we do that, we experience the joy of truly living—a joy that can only come from Him. What is the importance of Resurrection Sunday? It is the day that we celebrate our Savior's victory over death and sin. It is a day that we remember His great love for us. And it is a day that we recommit ourselves to living for Him.

How many days did Jesus stayed on earth after his resurrection?

After Jesus rose from the dead, he stayed on earth for 40 days. During that time, he appeared to many people and taught them about the Kingdom of God. He also told his disciples to spread the good news of the gospel to all the world. On the 40th day, Jesus ascended into heaven, and the disciples were left to carry on his work.

What happens after Resurrection Sunday?

What happens after Resurrection Sunday? The story of Easter doesn't end with Jesus' resurrection. In fact, the resurrection is just the beginning of the good news that we have to share with others. After Jesus rose from the dead, he appeared to his disciples and gave them instructions to go into all the world and preach the gospel. This is the message that we have been given to share with others: that Jesus is alive and that he offers forgiveness and new life to all who believe in him. The resurrection of Jesus changes everything. It means that death is no longer the end, and that we have hope for the future. It means that we can be forgiven and that we have a new relationship with God. The resurrection is good news for everyone. It is a message of hope that we can share with others.

How do we celebrate resurrection?

The word "Easter" is derived from Old English and originally referred to the Spring season. Over time, Easter became associated with the Christian holiday celebrating the resurrection of Jesus Christ. The holiday falls on the first Sunday following the first Full Moon after the Spring equinox. There are many different ways that Christians around the world celebrate the resurrection of Jesus Christ. Some Christians observe a period of fasting and prayer leading up to Easter Sunday. On Easter Sunday, many Christians attend church services and celebrate with special meals. Some Christians also give gifts, such as Easter eggs, to symbolize new life. The celebration of Easter is a joyous occasion for many Christians. It is a time to come together and celebrate the hope of new life.

Did Jesus come back to life on Easter Sunday?

Did Jesus come back to life on Easter Sunday? A common question with not-so-common answers. Some say yes, some say no – and there are many interpretations in between. But what does the Bible actually say? The Bible tells us that Jesus died on the cross and was buried. Matthew 27:57-60 says, "When it was evening, there came a rich man from Arimathea, named Joseph, who also was a disciple of Jesus. He went to Pilate and asked for the body of Jesus. Then Pilate ordered it to be given to him. And when Joseph had taken the body, he wrapped it in a clean linen cloth, and laid it in his own new tomb, which he had hewn out in the rock. He then rolled a great stone to the door of the tomb and went away." However, the story doesn't end there. On the third day, Easter Sunday, Jesus rose from the dead! The Bible tells us in Matthew 28:1-10, "After the Sabbath, at dawn on the first day of the week, Mary Magdalene and the other Mary went to look at the tomb. There was a severe earthquake, for an angel of the Lord descended from heaven, rolled back the stone, and sat on it. His appearance was like lightning, and his clothing was as white as snow. The guards were so afraid of him that they shook and became like dead men. The angel said to the women, "Do not be afraid, for I know that you are looking for Jesus, who was crucified. He is not here; he has risen, just as he said. Come and see the place where he lay. Then go quickly and tell his disciples: 'He has risen from the dead and is going ahead of you into Galilee.' There you will see him. Now I have told you." So the women hurried away from the tomb, afraid yet filled with joy, and ran to tell his disciples. Suddenly Jesus met them. "Greetings," he said. They came to him, clasped his feet and worshiped him. Then Jesus said to them, "Do not be afraid. Go and tell my brothers to go to Galilee; there they will see me." Did Jesus come back to life on Easter Sunday? The Bible tells us that he did! And not only that, but he fulfilled his promise to meet his disciples in Galilee. So whether you believe it or not, the answer is clear – Jesus did come back to life on Easter Sunday, just as he said he would.

What did Jesus do during the 40 days after the resurrection?

After Jesus rose from the dead, He appeared to many people over a period of 40 days. He appeared to the disciples on several occasions, as well as to His mother Mary. He also appeared to more than 500 people at once on one occasion. All of these appearances served to prove that He was truly alive and to give further instruction to His followers. One of the most significant things that Jesus did during this time was to commission His disciples to spread the gospel message to all nations. He told them that they would receive power when the Holy Spirit came upon them, and that they would be His witnesses in Jerusalem, in all Judea and Samaria, and to the ends of the earth. This commissioning of the disciples was the beginning of the Church's mission to evangelize the world. Another important thing that Jesus did during this time was to open the disciples' minds to understand the Scriptures. He explained to them how the Old Testament prophecies pointed to Him as the Messiah. He also taught them about His kingdom, which is not of this world. This understanding was essential for the disciples as they went out into the world to proclaim the gospel. Through His appearances and His teaching, Jesus made it abundantly clear that He was alive and that He had conquered death. He also showed His followers that He was still in control and that His kingdom was still advancing. The 40 days after the resurrection were a time of great joy and excitement for the disciples, and they were filled with the hope and the knowledge that Jesus was alive and that He was still in charge.

As Christians around the world celebrate Easter, the true meaning of the holiday can get lost in the Bunny, the baskets and the eggs. Easter is the day that we celebrate the resurrection of Jesus Christ. It is a time to reflect on his sacrifice and to remember that he conquered death so that we may have eternal life. It is a time to celebrate new beginnings and to be thankful for the many blessings that we have been given.

What is the Easter Bunny's name?

There are a lot of different stories about the Easter Bunny's name. One story says that the Easter Bunny's name is Peter Cottontail. This story comes from a book that was written in the 1950s. Another story says that the Easter Bunny's name is Hiram. This story comes from a book that was written in the 1800s. Hiram is a male name, so this story is probably not true. The most popular story about the Easter Bunny's name is that the Easter Bunny does not have a name. This story comes from a book that was written in the 1900s. This story is probably true because the Easter Bunny is a mythological creature.

What are the 7 words of Good Friday?

On Good Friday, we remember the seven last words that Jesus spoke from the cross. These words give us a glimpse into the heart of Christ and his great love for us. "Father, forgive them, for they know not what they do." Luke 23:34. Jesus spoke these words even as he was being crucified. He asked the Father to forgive those who were responsible for his death, even though they didn't know what they were doing. This shows us the great lengths that Jesus was willing to go to in order to forgive us. "Truly, I say to you, today you will be with me in Paradise." Luke 23:43. Jesus spoke these words to the thief who was being crucified next to him. Even in the midst of his pain and suffering, Jesus was thinking of others. He promised the thief that he would be with him in Paradise, showing us that he is always thinking of our eternal salvation. "Woman, behold, your son." John 19:26. These words were spoken to Mary, the mother of Jesus. As he was dying on the cross, Jesus made sure to take care of his mother. He knew that she would need someone to take care of her after he was gone, and so he entrusted her to the care of his disciple John. "My God, my God, why have you forsaken me?" Matthew 27:46. These are the words that Jesus cried out from the cross. He felt the weight of our sin and the separation from God that it caused. But even in that moment, he did not forsake us. He took our sin upon himself so that we could be forgiven. "I thirst." John 19:28. These are the words that Jesus spoke when he was incredibly thirsty. He had been on the cross for hours, and yet he was still thinking of our needs. He knew that we would be thirsty too, and so he asked for a drink. "It is finished." John 19:30. These are the words that Jesus spoke just before he died. He had completed the work that the Father had given him to do. He had taken our sin upon himself and paid the price for it. He had defeated death and conquered the grave. "Father, into your hands I commit my spirit." Luke 23:46. These are the last words that Jesus spoke before he died. He committed himself into the care of his Father, knowing that he was in good hands. The seven last words of Jesus show us his great love for us. He was willing to forgive those who crucified him, to take care of his mother, to suffer the consequences of our sin, and to die so that we could be forgiven. These words give us hope and comfort in knowing that Jesus loves us no matter what.

What did Jesus do on Good Friday?

On Good Friday, we remember the day that Jesus died on the cross. Jesus was crucified because he claimed to be the Son of God and the King of the Jews. The Romans crucified him because they saw this as a threat to their power. People often ask what Jesus did on Good Friday. The answer is that he died. He was tortured and then killed in a most brutal way. But his death was not the end. Three days later, he rose from the dead and showed himself to his disciples. His death and resurrection changed everything. Because of what he did, we can have forgiveness for our sins and a new life. If you have never believed in Jesus, Good Friday is a day to consider his claims and what he did for you.

What are you supposed to do on Good Friday?

According to the Christian tradition, Good Friday is the day on which Jesus Christ was crucified. Christians believe that Jesus was crucified because he claimed to be the Son of God, and his death was a sacrificial act that paid for the sins of humanity. Although Jesus died on Good Friday, Christians believe that he did not stay dead; he rose from the dead on Easter Sunday, proving his divinity and giving hope to Christians that they too will have eternal life. So, what are Christians supposed to do on Good Friday? Many Christians choose to spend the day in prayer and contemplation, reflecting on the events of Jesus' last days and on his sacrifice for humanity. Some churches hold special services on Good Friday, and some Christians attend these services. Others may choose to spend time reading the Bible or other religious texts, or perhaps visiting a place of Christian pilgrimage such as the Holy Land. Some Christians also choose to observe a fast on Good Friday, as a way of remembering Jesus' suffering and death. This can be a total fast, during which no food or drink is consumed, or it can be a partial fast, in which only certain types of food are avoided. Fasting is not required on Good Friday, but it is a popular practice among many Christians. Whatever you choose to do on Good Friday, the important thing is to remember what this day represents in the Christian faith. Good Friday is a day of mourning for Jesus' death, but also a day of hope, because we remember that Jesus conquered death and offers us eternal life.

What are 10 facts about Easter?

Easter is a holiday rooted in Christianity that celebrates the resurrection of Jesus Christ. It is typically observed through special church services,Observing lent, the decorating of Easter eggs and giving Easter baskets. Here are 10 facts about this special day: Easter falls on the first Sunday after the first full moon of the Spring season. Easter is also known as Pascha, which is Greek for "passover." Christians believe that Jesus rose from the dead on Easter Sunday, which is why the holiday is celebrated. The original Easter Bunny was a German creation. The first chocolate Easter eggs were made in Germany in the early 1800s. According to the Bible, Jesus' resurrection occurred on the third day after his crucifixion. The date of Easter changes every year because it is based on the lunar calendar. The word "Easter" is derived from the German word for "east," which is where the sun rises. Easter is the most important holiday in Christianity. In some Spanish-speaking countries, Easter is known as "Semana Santa," which means "holy week."

What is the story of Easter?

The story of Easter is one that is sometimes told as a fairy tale, but the true story is much more interesting. It all started with a man named Jesus who was born in a stable in Bethlehem. He was a very special child, and people soon began to follow him. As he got older, Jesus started teaching people about love, forgiveness, and peace. He also did some amazing things, like healing the sick and feeding the hungry. But not everyone liked what Jesus was saying. Some people thought he was a threat to their power, and they had him arrested. At his trial, Jesus was convicted of a crime he didn't commit and was sentenced to die on the cross. But even death couldn't stop him, and three days later Jesus rose from the dead. For Christians, Easter is a very special holiday because it reminds us of Jesus' victory over death. It is a time to celebrate his life and what he accomplished. It is also a time to reflect on our own lives and how we can follow in his footsteps.

Who invented Easter and why?

Easter is celebrated by Christians all over the world to commemorate the resurrection of Jesus Christ. But who invented this holiday and why? The simple answer is that no one person invented Easter. Rather, it was a gradual process that started with the early Christians commemorating the death and resurrection of Christ. But as the holiday evolved, various traditions were added on by different cultures and peoples. For example, the tradition of Easter eggs is thought to have originated in ancient pagan celebrations. Eggs were a symbol of new life and fertility, so it made sense that they would be associated with the resurrection of Christ. The Easter Bunny is another tradition that was added on later. The exact origins of the Easter Bunny are unclear, but it is thought to havebeen brought over to America by German immigrants in the 1700s. So why do we celebrate Easter? For Christians, it is a time to remember and give thanks for the sacrifice that Jesus made for us. It is also a time of hope, as we remember that Jesus defeated death and rose again, offering us the promise of eternal life.

Easter is a holiday that is celebrated by Christians all over the world. It commemorates the resurrection of Jesus Christ and is a time of joy and hope for many people. Easter is a time to be with family, friends, and loved ones, and to celebrate the hope that Jesus brings to our lives.

What happened to Jesus in the days Easter?

When most people think of Easter, they think of bunnies, chocolate eggs, and maybe even a church service. But what many people don't know is that Easter is actually a religious holiday commemorating the death and resurrection of Jesus Christ. So what exactly happened to Jesus during those days? The story of Easter begins on what is known as Palm Sunday. On this day, Jesus rode into Jerusalem on a donkey while people waved palm branches and shouted Hosanna. The next day, Jesus went to the Temple and threw out the money changers, saying they had turned His Father's house into a den of thieves. The following day, Jesus was back at the Temple teaching when the chief priests and the elders questioned His authority. In response, Jesus told them a story about a man who had two sons. The first son said he would go work in the vineyard, but ended up not going. The second son said he wouldn't go, but then changed his mind and went. Jesus concluded by saying that the son who changed his mind and went to work was the one who was being obedient. Later that day, Jesus was on His way to Bethany with His disciples when He was approached by a woman who had been bleeding for twelve years. She touched the hem of His garment and was immediately healed. The next day, as Jesus was teaching in the Temple, the chief priests and the scribes looked for a way to trap Him in His words. They asked Him if it was right to pay taxes to Caesar. Jesus responded by saying, "Give to Caesar what is Caesar's, and to God what is God's." His answer pleased neither the religious leaders nor the Roman authorities. On Thursday of that week, Jesus celebrated the Passover meal with His disciples. This was the last meal He would eat before His death. During the meal, Jesus told His disciples that one of them would betray Him. He also said that

He would not eat again until the kingdom of God had come. After the meal, Jesus and His disciples went to the Mount of Olives. Jesus told them that they would all fall away because of Him that night, but Peter said he would never fall away. Jesus then predicted that Peter would deny Him three times before the cock crowed the next morning. As Jesus predicted, Peter did deny Him three times. And shortly after that, Judas Iscariot, one of the twelve disciples, betrayed Jesus with a kiss. Jesus was then arrested and led away to be tried by the Sanhedrin. The next day, Jesus was brought before Pontius Pilate, the governor of Judea. Pilate found no fault in Jesus, but the religious leaders pressured him to condemn Jesus. So Pilate washed his hands of the situation and had Jesus flogged. After Jesus was flogged, he

What was Jesus doing the Monday before Easter?

It's Monday morning, just a few days before Easter Sunday. Jesus is getting ready to go into Jerusalem for the final time. He knows that his time is short and he wants to make the most of it. Jesus spends the morning with his disciples, teaching them and preparing them for what is to come. He knows that they will be the ones to carry on his work after he is gone. He loves them deeply and wants them to be ready. Around noon, Jesus and his disciples sit down to eat together. This will be their last meal together and Jesus wants to make it special. He blesses the food and thanks God for it. Then he sits down and eats with his friends. After the meal is over, Jesus and his disciples head out into the city. They spend the afternoon walking around, talking to people and healing the sick. Everywhere they go, Jesus is greeted with love and admiration. As the day starts to wind down, Jesus and his disciples make their way to the Mount of Olives. This is where Jesus will pray and where he will be betrayed. As they stand on the mount, looking out over the city, Jesus speaks words of love and peace. He knows the difficulties that lie ahead, but he is ready to face them. And then, it is time for Jesus to go. He bids farewell to his disciples and heads into the city to meet his fate.

Why is Easter related to Jesus?

Easter is a religious holiday that celebrates the resurrection of Jesus Christ. The holiday is observed by Christians around the world and is one of the most important days in the Christian calendar. There are many theories about why Easter is related to Jesus. One theory is that Easter celebrates the new life that Jesus brought into the world. Another theory is that Easter is a symbol of hope and resurrection, and that by celebrating Easter, Christians are reminded of the hope that they have in Jesus. Whatever the reason, there is no doubt that Easter is a very important day for Christians, and that it is a day that is deeply rooted in the Christian faith. As Christians celebrate Easter, they are reminded of the hope that they have in Jesus Christ, and they are given a chance to reflect on the sacrifices that he made for them.

What are the eggs symbolic of in Easter?

There are many traditions that are associated with Easter, but one of the most prevalent is the decorating and hiding of eggs. For many, the eggs are simply a fun decoration to enjoy during the holiday. But for many Christians, the eggs hold a much deeper meaning. Eggs have long been a symbol of life. In many ancient cultures, they were seen as a representation of the soul. For Christians, this makes them the perfect symbol for Easter. Easter is a time to celebrate the resurrection of Jesus Christ and the new life that he brings. The eggs serve as a reminder of this new life. Easter eggs are often decorated with symbols of the faith. Crosses, doves, and lilies are all popular choices. These decorations serve as a reminder of the hope and joy that Easter brings. The eggs are also a reminder of the promises of eternal life that are found in the Christian faith. The hiding of the eggs is also significant. It is a reminder of the way that Christ was hidden from the world after his crucifixion. But just as the eggs are found, so too is Christ. This serves as a reminder that no one is ever lost to God. The eggs are just one of the many symbols that are associated with Easter. But for Christians, they are a reminder of the hope and joy that the holiday brings. They are a reminder of the new life that Jesus brings and the promises of eternal life that are found in the Christian faith.

Why do Jehovah's not celebrate Easter?

Easter is a religious holiday that commemorates the resurrection of Jesus Christ. For Christians, this is the most important holiday of the year. However, Jehovah's Witnesses do not celebrate Easter. There are a number of reasons for this. First, Jehovah's Witnesses believe that the Bible does not instruct Christians to celebrate Easter. They believe that the Bible clearly states that Christians should not follow the customs and traditions of pagans. Easter is a holiday that has its roots in paganism, and Jehovah's Witnesses believe that Christians should not partake in pagan celebrations. Second, Jehovah's Witnesses believe that the holiday of Easter is based on a false understanding of the Bible. They believe that the Bible does not teach that Jesus was resurrected on Easter Sunday. Instead, they believe that Jesus was resurrected on a Wednesday. Therefore, they do not see any reason to celebrate Easter on a Sunday. Third, Jehovah's Witnesses believe that the holiday of Easter has been corrupted by secularism. They believe that many of the customs and traditions associated with Easter, such as the Easter bunny and Easter eggs, are secular in nature and have nothing to do with the religious meaning of the holiday. Overall, there are a number of reasons why Jehovah's Witnesses do not celebrate Easter. They believe that the holiday is rooted in paganism, that it is based on a false understanding of the Bible, and that it has been corrupted by secularism.

Who created Easter?

Easter is a religious holiday celebrated by Christians around the world. The holiday commemorates the death and resurrection of Jesus Christ, and is considered by many to be the most important day of the Christian calendar. So who created Easter? The answer, like many religious questions, is complicated. The holiday of Easter actually has its roots in pagan celebrations of fertility and springtime. The word "Easter" is actually derived from the name of the Anglo-Saxon goddess of spring and fertility, Eastre. Christians believe that Jesus was crucified on Good Friday and rose from the dead on Easter Sunday. This event, known as the Resurrection, is considered to be the cornerstone of the Christian faith. The holiday of Easter is therefore a time for Christians to remember and celebrate the ultimate sacrifice that Jesus made for them. While the origins of Easter are pagan, the holiday was adopted by the early Christian church and given new meaning. For Christians, Easter is a time to reflect on the true meaning of the holiday – the sacrifice of Jesus Christ and his triumph over death.

What did Jesus say about Easter?

In the Christian tradition, Easter is a celebration of the resurrection of Jesus Christ. The holiday has its roots in ancient pagan celebrations of spring and new life. Christians believe that Jesus was crucified on Good Friday and rose from the dead on Easter Sunday. The Easter story is told in the Bible in the New Testament. The first account of the resurrection is in the Gospel of Matthew. In this account, Mary Magdalene and the other Mary go to the tomb of Jesus on the morning of the resurrection. They find the stone that had been rolled away from the tomb and an angel sitting on the stone. The angel tells them that Jesus has risen from the dead and that they should go and tell the disciples. The second account is in the Gospel of Mark. In this account, three women - Mary Magdalene, Mary the mother of James, and Salome - go to the tomb of Jesus. They find the stone rolled away and a young man dressed in a white robe sitting inside the tomb. The man tells them that Jesus has risen from the dead and that they should go and tell the disciples. The third account is in the Gospel of Luke. In this account, two women - Mary Magdalene and Joanna - go to the tomb of Jesus. They find the stone rolled away and the tomb empty. They go back and tell the disciples what they have seen. The fourth and final account of the resurrection is in the Gospel of John. In this account, Mary Magdalene goes to the tomb of Jesus. She finds the stone rolled away and the tomb empty. She goes back and tells the disciples what she has seen. So what did Jesus say about Easter? The answer is, we don't really know. The Bible doesn't record any words spoken by Jesus about Easter. This doesn't mean that Jesus didn't say anything about Easter. It simply means that the Bible doesn't record any of Jesus' words on the subject. What we do know is that Jesus died on the cross and rose from the dead. This is the central message of Christianity. This is what Easter is all about. Easter is a time to celebrate the Good News that Jesus is alive!

Easter is a religious holiday celebrated by Christians around the world. It commemorates the death and resurrection of Jesus Christ, and is considered the most important day in the Christian calendar. Catholics and Protestants have different traditions surrounding Easter, but the holiday is a time of joy and celebration for all Christians.

What religion does not believe in the resurrection?

What religion does not believe in the resurrection? There are a few religious groups that do not believe in the resurrection of the dead, including some sects of Judaism and Islam. Some Gnostic Christians also don't believe in it, although most Christians do. The belief in the resurrection of the dead is not essential to Christianity, as evidenced by the fact that there are Christians who don't believe in it. Paul of Tarsus, one of the most important early Christian figures, wrote in 1 Corinthians 15:12-19 that if there is no resurrection, then Christianity is worthless and believers are to be pitied more than anyone. So why do some religious groups not believe in the resurrection? There are a few different reasons. Some people interpret the biblical stories of Jesus' resurrection as allegories or symbols, rather than historical events. This was the view of the early Christian figure Origen, who said that the stories were true in a spiritual sense but not in a literal sense. Others believe that the concept of the resurrection contradicts scientific laws. For example, the British philosopher David Hume wrote that belief in the resurrection is "opposed to all experience" and is therefore "the most egregious instance of all superstition." Still others believe that the idea of the resurrection is simply too good to be true. As the French philosopher Jean-Paul Sartre put it, "if God does not exist, everything is permitted." If there is no afterlife, then there is no reason to believe in the resurrection. Whatever the reasons may be, there are certainly some religious groups that do not believe in the resurrection of the dead.

Why do Catholics believe in burying the dead?

Catholics believe in burying the dead because they believe in the resurrection of the body. When a person dies, their soul goes to heaven but their body remains on earth. Catholics believe that when Christ returns on Judgment Day, he will raise all of the dead and give them new bodies. This is why Catholics believe it is important to bury the dead rather than cremating them. Cremation destroys the body and makes it impossible for Christ to raise that person on Judgment Day.

Why did Christians change the Sabbath from Saturday to Sunday?

Many Christians dispute whether or not the Sabbath should be on Sunday, the day of the resurrection of Jesus Christ. The earliest Christians observed the Jewish Sabbath, which is Saturday. Christians did not change the Sabbath to Sunday worship until the late 2nd century. There are a few reasons why Christians may have made this change. Some say that Christians changed the day of worship to Sunday because that is the day that Jesus rose from the dead. On the first day of the week, when the women went to the tomb, they found that Jesus was not there. He had risen! Because of this, some Christians may have thought that Sunday should be the day of worship, as it is a reminder of the resurrection. Another reason Christians may have changed the day of worship to Sunday is because it is the day of the new creation. In Genesis, we see that God creates the world in six days and rested on the seventh. When Jesus rose from the dead, he created a new creation. Because of this, some Christians think that Sunday is the day of worship, as it is a reminder of the new creation. A third reason Christians may have changed the day of worship to Sunday is because it is the first day of the week. In the Bible, we see that God created the world on the first day of the week. Christians may have thought that Sunday should be the day of worship because it is the first day of the week and a reminder of the creation. Christians changed the Sabbath from Saturday to Sunday worship because of the resurrection of Jesus Christ, the new creation, or the first day of the week.

What was the main cause of Jesus death?

The main cause of Jesus' death was crucifixion. Crucifixion was a common method of execution in ancient Rome and was reserved for the worst criminals – slaves, traitors, and rebels. According to the Gospels, Jesus was sentenced to death by crucifixion because he claimed to be the Son of God and the King of the Jews. Although the exact details are unknown, crucifixion was a painful and humiliating death. Jesus was likely nailed to a wooden cross and left to die. The Gospels describe the crucifixion of Jesus as a public event that drew a large crowd. His execution was carried out by the Roman authorities, who were the occupying power in Judea at the time. The Gospels also describe Jesus as being mocked and ridiculed by the soldiers and the crowd as he died. The main cause of Jesus' death was crucifixion. This method of execution was reserved for the worst criminals – slaves, traitors, and rebels. Jesus was likely nailed to a wooden cross and left to die. The Gospels describe the crucifixion of Jesus as a public event that drew a large crowd. His execution was carried out by the Roman authorities, who were the occupying power in Judea at the time. The Gospels also describe Jesus as being mocked and ridiculed by the soldiers and the crowd as he died.

Which Bible verse talks about the death of Jesus?

The Bible verse that talks about the death of Jesus is John 3:16. It says, "For God so loved the world that he gave his one and only Son, that whoever believes in him shall not perish but have eternal life."

How Jesus was crucified?

How was Jesus crucified? The crucifixion of Jesus is one of the most important events in history. It is the central story of Christianity, and is remembered and celebrated every year on Easter Sunday. But how exactly did Jesus die? The answer may surprise you. The Bible tells us that Jesus was crucified by being nailed to a cross. However, the word "crucifixion" does not appear in the Bible. This is because the word was not used in ancient times. The word only began to be used in the Middle Ages, long after the events of the New Testament. The word "cross" is first used in the Bible in the book of Genesis. There, we read that Abraham was prepared to sacrifice his son Isaac on a mountain. But God intervened and provided a ram to be sacrificed instead. The cross was also used as a symbol by the ancient Egyptians and the Persians. But it was the Romans who first used it as a means of execution. Crucifixion was a punishment reserved for the worst criminals. It was a slow and painful death. The victim would be nailed or tied to a cross and left to die. The Romans did not invent crucifixion, but they perfected it. They used it as a way to discourage rebellion and to send a message to the populace that the state had absolute power. In the first century AD, the Roman empire was the most powerful force in the world. And the crucifixion of Jesus would have been seen as a challenge to that power. Jesus was arrested and tried by the Roman authorities. He was found guilty of sedition and sentenced to death. The Romans would have seen the crucifixion of Jesus as a way to send a message that anyone who challenged their power would meet the same fate. Jesus was crucified between two thieves. This was not unusual. It was common for criminals to be crucified together. The crucifixion of Jesus would have been a public event. It would have been meant to discourage anyone else from challenging Roman authority. However, the story of Jesus did not end with his crucifixion. Three days after his death, Jesus rose from the dead. This event changed the course of history. It is the reason that we celebrate Easter today. The crucifixion of Jesus was a brutal and painful death. But it was also the beginning of a new life for all who believe in him.

Why did Jesus give up his life for us?

It is often said that Jesus died for our sins. But what does that really mean? Why would Jesus sacrifice his life if it wasn't absolutely necessary? The Bible tells us that Jesus came to Earth as a ransom for many. In other words, his death was a substitutionary sacrifice. He died in our place so that we could be forgiven and have eternal life. But why did Jesus have to die? If God is all-powerful, couldn't he just forgive us without requiring a death? The answer has to do with the character of God. He is both just and merciful. As a just God, he must punish sin. But as a merciful God, he also desires to forgive. So how can these two attributes of God be reconciled? The answer is the cross. On the cross, Jesus took on the punishment that we deserve. He died in our place. And because he is God, his death was enough to atone for all the sins of the world. In other words, Jesus died for our sins because that is what it took to restore our relationship with God. It was the only way that our sin could be forgiven and we could be made right with God. And that is good news. Because it means that we don't have to pay the penalty for our own sin. We can be forgiven and have eternal life because of what Jesus did for us on the cross.

Easter is a time to remember the sacrifice of Jesus Christ and the hope that His resurrection brings to Christians. It is also a time for families and friends to get together, enjoy time together, and eat lots of good food!

How old was Jesus when he was crucified?

How old was Jesus when he was crucified? This is a difficult question to answer definitively as there is no record of Jesus' age at the time of his crucifixion in the Bible. However, based on the account of his birth in the Gospels of Luke and Matthew, Jesus was most likely between the ages of 30 and 33 when he was crucified. The Gospel of Luke tells us that Jesus was "about thirty years old" when he began his public ministry (Luke 3:23). This would put him at the age of 33 when he was crucified, as his ministry is thought to have lasted around three years. The Gospel of Matthew, on the other hand, tells us that Jesus was born when Herod the Great was ruling over Judea (Matthew 2:1). Herod died in 4 BCE, which would mean that Jesus was between 27 and 30 years old when he was crucified. So, based on the accounts of his birth in the Gospels of Luke and Matthew, Jesus was most likely between the ages of 30 and 33 when he was crucified.

What was Jesus Last saying before he died?

"It is finished," Jesus said with a loud voice, and then he breathed his last. With those words, he gave up his spirit. It was early morning, and the sky was just starting to lighten up. The sun had not yet risen, but the birds were already singing. Jesus was hanging on the cross, and he had been there for hours. He was in a lot of pain, and his body was covered in blood. The people who had gathered to watch him die were jeering and laughing at him. They were glad that he was suffering. Some of them were even throwing things at him. Jesus had been arrested because he had claimed to be the King of the Jews. But the Jewish leaders did not believe him, and they sent him to the Roman authorities to be put to death. The Roman soldiers had tortured him before they crucified him. They had beaten him and put a crown of thorns on his head. They had mocked him and called him names. Now, Jesus was hanging on the cross between two thieves. His eyes were full of sadness, but there was also a look of peace. He had forgiven those who had crucified him. He had asked God to forgive them, because he knew that they didn't know what they were doing. Jesus had suffered the punishment for our sins. He had died in our place. And now, he was saying that it was finished. The work that he had come to do was complete. He had given his life for us, and there was nothing more that he could do. When Jesus said, "It is finished," he was not just talking about his life. He was also talking about our salvation. He had paid the price for our sins, and now we can have eternal life. We can have a relationship with God. All we need to do is to believe in Jesus and ask him to forgive us.

What words did Jesus say before he died?

On the night before he died, Jesus gathered his closest disciples around him and shared some of his final words. Here are some of the things he said, as recorded in the Bible: "Do not let your hearts be troubled. You believe in God; believe also in me. My Father's house has many rooms; if that were not so, would I have told you that I am going there to prepare a place for you? And if I go and prepare a place for you, I will come back and take you to be with me that you also may be where I am. You know the way to the place where I am going." (John 14:1-4) "I am the way and the truth and the life. No one comes to the Father except through me. If you really know me, you will know my Father as well. From now on, you do know him and have seen him." (John 14:6-7) "Peace I leave with you; my peace I give you. I do not give to you as the world gives. Do not let your hearts be troubled and do not be afraid." (John 14:27) "I have told you these things, so that in me you may have peace. In this world you will have trouble. But take heart! I have overcome the world." (John 16:33) "Now is your time of grief, but I will see you again and you will rejoice, and no one will take away your joy." (John 16:22) "Father, into your hands I commit my spirit." (Luke 23:46) These are just some of the things Jesus said in his final hours. What is clear from all of his words is that he was not afraid of death, and he wanted his disciples to know that they need not be afraid either. He also wanted them to know that he was going to prepare a place for them in heaven, and that he would one day return to take them there. Finally, he wanted them to know that despite the troubles they would face in this world, they could take heart because he had overcome the world.

What did Jesus say at his death?

What did Jesus say at his death? "Father, forgive them, for they know not what they do" (Luke 23:34). With these words, Jesus Christ showed us the power of forgiveness, even in the face of death. He also asked God to have mercy on those who were responsible for his execution, even though they did not fully understand what they were doing. Jesus' final words were a prayer for God's forgiveness, not only for those who were putting him to death, but also for all of humanity. In this moment, Jesus recognized that our entire world is in need of forgiveness, and he was willing to offer that forgiveness even at the cost of his own life. What an incredible display of love! Jesus' final words also show us the importance of always seeking forgiveness. When we wrong someone, it is never too late to ask for their forgiveness. No matter how big or small our transgressions may be, we can always find forgiveness by turning to Jesus.

How long was Jesus alive after his crucifixion?

The debate surrounding the length of time Jesus lived after his crucifixion revolves around a few key scriptures. One key scripture is John 20:1-10, which says that on the first day of the week, Mary Magdalene came to the tomb early in the morning, while it was still dark, and saw the stone that had been removed from the tomb.She then saw two angels in white sitting where Jesus' body had been, one at the head and one at the feet. They asked her why she was crying, and she replied that she was looking for Jesus. She turned around and saw Jesus standing there, but she didn't recognize him at first. He asked her why she was crying, and she told him that she thought he was the gardener. He then said her name, "Mary," and she finally realized that it was Jesus. He told her not to touch him because he had not yet ascended to his Father. Another key scripture is Acts 1:3, which says that after his suffering, Jesus presented himself alive to his disciples by many convincing proofs. He appeared to them over a period of forty days and spoke about the kingdom of God. So, how long was Jesus alive after his crucifixion? The answer depends on how you interpret the key scriptures. If you take John 20:1-10 as a literal account, then Jesus was alive for at least three days after his crucifixion. If you interpret Acts 1:3 as a reference to Jesus' entire ministry, then Jesus was alive for over forty days after his crucifixion. There are many different interpretations of the key scriptures, but ultimately, it is up to each individual to decide what they believe.

How heavy was Jesus cross?

How heavy was Jesus' cross? This is a question that has been asked throughout history, with no definitive answer. Some say that the cross was incredibly heavy, while others claim that it was relatively light. One theory is that the cross was so heavy that Jesus could hardly carry it. This would explain why Simon of Cyrene was asked to help Jesus carry the cross. However, this theory has been met with criticism, as some argue that if the cross was so heavy, Simon would have also struggled to carry it. Another theory is that the cross was relatively light. This is based on the fact that Jesus was able to carry it for a good distance before collapsing. This theory is supported by the fact that Roman soldiers were often required to carry heavy loads, and thus would have been able to carry a heavier cross than most people. So, what is the answer? Unfortunately, there is no way to know for sure. However, both theories have some merit, and it is likely that the truth lies somewhere in between. No matter how heavy the cross was, it was clearly a burden for Jesus, and something that he would have preferred not to have to carry.

Who took Jesus off the cross?

Who took Jesus off the cross? This is a question that has puzzled historians and theologians for centuries. There is no certain answer, and there are a number of theories that have been put forward. One theory is that Joseph of Arimathea, a wealthy follower of Jesus, asked for his body after the crucifixion and took it down from the cross. This is the theory that is most often portrayed in art and literature. Another theory is that the Roman soldiers who were tasked with carrying out the crucifixion were the ones who took Jesus down from the cross. This is because they would have needed to remove the bodies of the crucified victims before they could be taken away for burial. Whatever the case may be, we do know that Jesus' body was taken down from the cross and that he was buried in a tomb. His body was never found, and his tomb was found empty a few days later. This led to the belief that Jesus had risen from the dead, which is a central tenet of Christianity.

The religious holiday of Easter is celebrated by Christians all over the world. It commemorates the resurrection of Jesus Christ and is a time of hope and renewal. For many, it is a day of family, food, and fun. Easter is a special time to come together and celebrate life.

Did Jesus know he would be crucified?

There is no easy answer to the question of whether or not Jesus knew he would be crucified. The Bible does not give a direct answer, and scholars have long debated the issue. On one hand, it seems unlikely that Jesus would have allowed himself to be arrested and put to death if he had known what was going to happen. He was, after all, God incarnate, and could have easily stopped the whole process if he had wanted to. On the other hand, Jesus was a human being as well as a divine being, and it is possible that he did know what was going to happen to him. In the Garden of Gethsemane, for example, he is said to have been in agony, and even asked God to let the cup pass from him (Luke 22:39-46). It is also worth noting that Jesus predicted his own death on several occasions (Matthew 16:21, 17:22-23, 20:17-19), which would seem to indicate that he knew what was going to happen. So what is the answer? Did Jesus know he was going to be crucified? The truth is, we don't really know. But what we do know is that, regardless of whether he knew or not, he went ahead and allowed it to happen. He did so because he loved us, and wanted to save us from our sins.

What is the Holy Spirit?

The Holy Spirit is one of the three aspects of the Triune God and is considered to be the Third Person of the Trinity. Although the word "Trinity" is not found in the Bible, it is a concept that is essential to understanding the nature of God. The doctrine of the Trinity teaches that there is one God in three Persons, namely, the Father, the Son, and the Holy Spirit. This means that the Holy Spirit is not a separate being from the Father and the Son, but is rather the Spirit of God. The word "spirit" in Hebrew can be understood in two ways. First, it can be seen as an invisible force or power, such as when the Spirit of God is said to have "hovered over the waters" in Genesis 1:2. Second, the word "spirit" can also refer to a person's character or inner being. In the Bible, the Holy Spirit is often spoken of as being like a person, with a will and emotions. For example, in Acts 5:3-4, Peter says to Ananias, "Why has Satan filled your heart to lie to the Holy Spirit?" Here, it is clear that the Holy Spirit is not just an invisible power, but is a personal being. The term "Holy Spirit" is used in a number of ways in the Bible. Sometimes it is used to refer to the invisible power of God, as in Acts 1:8, where it says that the disciples would be "baptized in the Holy Spirit not many days from now." In other passages, the term is used to refer to the Third Person of the Trinity. For example, in Matthew 28:19, Jesus says, "Go therefore and make disciples of all the nations, baptizing them in the name of the Father and of the Son and of the Holy Spirit." Here, it is clear that the Holy Spirit is distinct from the Father and the Son, but is also equal to them. The Holy Spirit is often spoken of as the one who convicts us of sin and leads us to repentance. In John 16:8, Jesus says, "And when He has come, He will convict the world of sin, and of righteousness, and of judgment." The Holy Spirit is also the one who gives us spiritual gifts, as in 1 Corinthians 12:4-11. These gifts are given to us for the building up of the body of Christ and the furtherance of the gospel. The Holy Spirit is an important part of who God is, and He has an important role in our lives as well. He convicts us of our sin and leads us to repentance, and He gives us spiritual gifts to help us in our walk with Christ. We need to be mindful of the Holy Spirit and ask for His help and guidance in our lives.

Why did God sacrifice his Son?

When we think about Easter, the first thing that comes to mind is usually the Easter bunny and chocolate eggs. But Easter is actually a religious holiday that commemorates the death and resurrection of Jesus Christ. So why did God sacrifice his Son? There are a few different interpretations of this, but the most common one is that it was an act of love. God loved us so much that he was willing to sacrifice his Son in order to save us from our sins. Another interpretation is that it was a way for God to show us how much he values life. by sacrificing his Son, God was showing us that life is more important than anything else. And finally, some people believe that the sacrifice of Jesus was a way for God to show us that we are never alone. Even when we feel like we are at our lowest, God is always there with us. So, why did God sacrifice his Son? There is no one answer to that question. But whatever the reason, it was an act of love, and it is something that we should remember and be thankful for every Easter.

What was Jesus last name?

What was Jesus last name? This is a question that has been asked throughout history, with no clear answer. Some say that Jesus didn't have a last name, while others say that his last name was Christ. There is no clear evidence to support either claim. The Bible doesn't give a clear answer to this question. In the book of Mark, Jesus is only referred to as "Jesus Christ", without a last name. However, in the book of John, Jesus is referred to as "Jesus of Nazareth". This could suggest that his last name was Christ, but it is not definitive. Some scholars believe that Christ was not Jesus' last name, but rather a title. This is supported by the fact that "Christ" is not a name that would have been given to someone in Jesus' time. The word "Christ" comes from the Greek word Christos, which means "anointed one". This was a title that was given to someone who was seen as being special or chosen by God. So, what was Jesus' last name? We may never know for sure. But what we do know is that he was a special person who was chosen by God to spread his message of love and forgiveness.

What language did Jesus speak?

Most scholars agree that Jesus was a Galilean who spoke Aramaic, the common language of that region. However, there is some debate as to what language he spoke during his crucifixion. The Gospels of Mark and Matthew say that Jesus was mocked by the soldiers for speaking Aramaic, while the Gospel of John claims that he spoke Hebrew. It is possible that Jesus spoke a mix of languages, depending on the situation. Aramaic was the common language of Galilee, but Hebrew was the language of scripture and prayer. Jesus may have spoken Aramaic to his disciples and Hebrew to the crowds. We don't know for sure what language Jesus spoke, but it is likely that he was bilingual in Aramaic and Hebrew. This would have allowed him to communicate with people from all walks of life. Some scholars believe that Jesus also spoke Greek, as this was the lingua franca of the Mediterranean region. Greek was the language of the Roman Empire and would have been helpful for Jesus if he wanted to spread his message to a wider audience. We will never know for sure what language Jesus spoke, but it is clear that he was a master of communication. He was able to connect with people from all backgrounds and communicate his message in a way that everyone could understand.

How tall was Jesus?

There is no historical record of Jesus's height, so any answer to this question is simply an educated guess. The average height for a man in Jesus's time is thought to have been about 5 feet 5 inches, but this can vary considerably depending on the region. Some people believe that Jesus was significantly taller than the average man, as he is often depicted as such in art. One theory is that artists subconsciously made Jesus taller than average to convey His importance. There is also the possibility that Jesus was shorter than average. This may have been due to the fact that He lived in a time and place where food was scarce and people were often malnourished. The Bible does not give us a definite answer as to how tall Jesus was, but we can make some educated guesses based on the available evidence. Regardless of His actual height, Jesus was a man of great importance whose teachings have impacted billions of people throughout history.

What was the 2nd word of Jesus on the cross?

When Jesus was on the cross, his final words were "Father, forgive them, for they know not what they do." Some people believe that the second word he said was "today," but there is no evidence to support this claim. It is more likely that he said "Father" first and then "forgive them." Either way, his final words were about forgiveness and love.

Although the Easter holiday has Pagan origins, it has become a significant religious holiday for Christians around the world. Every year, millions of people celebrate the resurrection of Jesus Christ, and the holiday is a time of hope and renewal. For many, Easter is a time to come together with family and friends, and to celebrate the joys of spring.

How many times did Jesus cry on the cross?

On the cross, Jesus cries out twice: once with a loud voice and once with a quiet voice. In the loud voice, he cries out, "My God, my God, why have you forsaken me?" This is a quotation from Psalm 22, which is a psalm of lament. In the quiet voice, he utters the words, "Into your hands I commit my spirit." Both of these utterances are significant. The loud cry is a cry of anguish, of abandonment. It is a cry that echoes the feelings of the psalmist in Psalm 22. The quiet cry is a cry of surrender, of trust. It is a cry that Jesus makes without any words of complaint or anger. He simply surrenders himself to God. The two cries of Jesus on the cross reveal the depths of his love for us. In his loud cry, we see his humanness, his empathy, his solidarity with us in our suffering. In his quiet cry, we see his divinity, his trust in God, his submission to God's will. Through his cries, we see that Jesus is both fully human and fully divine. The two cries of Jesus on the cross also reveal the depths of our sinfulness. In his loud cry, we see the result of our sinfulness, the separation from God that our sin causes. In his quiet cry, we see the grace of God, the willingness of God to receive us even in our sinfulness. Through his cries, we see that our sinfulness is both real and forgiven. The two cries of Jesus on the cross teach us that we can come to God with both our sorrow and our joy, with both our agony and our ecstasy. We can come to God with our loud cries and our quiet cries. We can come to God with all that we are, and all that we are not. And God will receive us.

What were Jesus last 3 words?

What were Jesus last 3 words? "It is finished." With these words, Jesus Christ brought His earthly mission to a close. He had come to save His people from their sins, and He had done just that. He had taught them, healed them, and loved them. And now, He was going to die for them. What did these three little words mean? First and foremost, they meant that Jesus had completed the task He had been sent to do. He had finished His work of redemption. He had paid the price for our sins, and He had been raised from the dead, as He had promised. These words also meant that all of God's promises to His people had now been fulfilled. all of the Old Testament prophecies about the Messiah had been fulfilled in Jesus. He was the long-awaited Savior, and He had come to save His people from their sin. Lastly, these words meant that Jesus was now ready to return to His Father. He had accomplished everything He had set out to do, and He was now ready to go home. What a comfort it is to know that Jesus finished the work of salvation! He did not leave us alone to face our sin and our death. He has conquered sin and death, and He offers us life and peace. When we hear those three little words, "It is finished," let us remember that our salvation is secure in Jesus Christ. We can have confidence in His finished work, and we can rest assured that He will never leave us or forsake us. Thanks be to God for His amazing grace!

Why did Jesus cry on the cross?

On the night Jesus was betrayed, he offered a prayer to God. "Father, if you are willing, take this cup from me; yet not my will, but yours be done" (Luke 22:42). In this prayer, Jesus was expressing his human desire to avoid the coming suffering. He knew what was going to happen and he didn't want to go through with it. But he was willing to submit to God's will. So why did Jesus cry on the cross? There are a few possible reasons. First, Jesus may have wept because of the pain he was experiencing. The Bible says that Jesus was beaten beyond recognition (Isaiah 52:14). He was mocked, spat on, and had a crown of thorns shoved onto his head. The physical pain would have been unbearable. Second, Jesus may have wept because of the spiritual pain he was experiencing. On the cross, Jesus took on the sins of the world (2 Corinthians 5:21). He became our substitute, bearing the punishment we deserved. The weight of our sin was crushing him. Third, Jesus may have wept because he felt forsaken by his Father. When Jesus cried out, "My God, my God, why have you forsaken me?" (Psalm 22:1), he was quoting from a psalm that expressed the anguish of being abandoned by God. As far as we can tell, this was the only time Jesus ever felt forsaken by his Father. And he felt it at the moment when he needed him the most. Fourth, Jesus may have wept because he was thinking of all the people who would never repent and receive forgiveness. He loved sinners and he came to die for them (Luke 19:10). And yet, he knew that many would never repent and come to faith. The thought of all those who would perish in their sin must have been agonizing for him. Finally, Jesus may have wept because he was looking ahead to the joy of the resurrection. He knew that his suffering was only temporary and that he would soon be reunited with his Father in heaven. The resurrection was the goal of his mission and it was worth the cost of his life. We don't know for sure why Jesus wept on the cross. But whatever the reason, his tears show us that he was fully human. He felt pain, anguish, and doubt. He faced temptation and suffering. And yet, he was willing to go through with it because he loved us and he trusted his Father.

Why did Jesus pray before his death?

When Jesus was on the cross, He prayed, "Father, forgive them, for they know not what they do" (Luke 23:34). He also prayed, "My God, My God, why have You forsaken Me?" (Matthew 27:46). Finally, He said, "It is finished" (John 19:30). Why did Jesus pray before His death? There are a few possible explanations. First, Jesus was taught to pray. As a Jew, He would have been raised with the idea that prayer is important. Second, Jesus was human. He was about to die a painful and humiliating death. It makes sense that He would pray for strength and for God's help. Third, Jesus was God's Son. He had a special relationship with God. Even though He was about to die, He continued to trust in God and to seek His will. Fourth, Jesus knew that His death would have a great impact on the world. He prayed for God's forgiveness for those who killed Him and for God's help for those who would follow Him. Fifth, Jesus' death was the fulfillment of God's plan. He had come to die for the sins of the world. By His death, He would make a way for anyone who believes in Him to have eternal life. Jesus prayed before He died because He loved us and He wanted us to know that God hears our prayers.

Where did Jesus go between his death and resurrection?

When Jesus died on the cross, his spirit left his body and descended into the realm of the dead. There, he preached to the spirits who had not yet been able to accept the gospel. He also continued his work of atoning for their sins, as he had done for all humanity while he was alive. After he had finished his work in the spirit world, Jesus returned to his body and was resurrected. He then ascended into heaven, where he sits at the right hand of the Father. From there, he will return to earth to judge the living and the dead.

Where did Jesus go when he died?

entertainment Did you ever wonder where Jesus went when he died? No, not heaven. I'm referring to the three days in between his death and resurrection. According to the Bible, Jesus spent this time in hell. Now, I know what you're thinking. How could a loving and just God send His own Son to hell? Well, He didn't do it for punishment. God didn't condemn Jesus, because He is unable to do so. His justice and holiness demand that sin be punished, but instead of punishing Jesus, God punished Him by giving Him what we deserved. So, what did Jesus do in hell? The Bible doesn't give us a lot of details, but we do know that He preached to the spirits in prison (1 Peter 3:18-20). He also went as a victorious conqueror, because His death and resurrection conquered sin and death once and for all (Hebrews 2:14-15). In the end, it doesn't really matter where Jesus went when He died. What matters is that He died for you and me. He took our punishment upon Himself, so that we could be forgiven and have eternal life. That is the Good News of the gospel!

Where is the crown of thorns?

The crown of thorns is a symbol of the crucifixion of Jesus Christ and is considered to be one of the most important relics in Christianity. It is believed to have been placed on Jesus' head during the crucifixion, and is often depicted in artwork and Archaeology. The relic is currently located in the Notre Dame Cathedral in Paris, France. The crown of thorns is a symbol of the suffering of Jesus Christ and his sacrifice for humanity. It is a reminder of the important role that Jesus played in the Christian faith. The crown of thorns also represents the victory of Jesus over death. The relic of the crown of thorns is located in the Notre Dame Cathedral in Paris, France. The cathedral is a major tourist attraction in the city, and the relic is one of the most popular pieces of artwork in the cathedral. The crown of thorns is kept in a reliquary, which is a type of container used to store relics. The reliquary is made of gold and silver, and is decorated with images of Jesus and the Virgin Mary. The crown of thorns is an important symbol in Christianity, and is a reminder of the sacrifice that Jesus made for humanity. The relic is located in the Notre Dame Cathedral in Paris, France, and is one of the most popular pieces of artwork in the cathedral.

Easter is a time for many people to celebrate the life and teachings of Jesus Christ. For others, it is a time to simply enjoy the spring season. No matter how you choose to spend your Easter, we hope you have a blessed day!

How tall was the Virgin Mary?

The question of the Virgin Mary's height has been a matter of debate for centuries. Some say she was tall, while others argue she was of average height. There is no clear consensus on this matter. The Bible does not give a clear indication of the Virgin Mary's height. However, there are a few passages that suggest she may have been tall. In the book of Revelation, Mary is described as being 'clothed in a robe reaching to her feet' (Revelation 12:1). This would suggest that she was at least of average height, if not taller. There are also a number of artistic depictions of the Virgin Mary that show her to be tall. For example, in the painting 'The Annunciation' by Fra Angelico, Mary is shown to be significantly taller than the angel Gabriel. This suggests that the artist believed her to be tall. However, there are also many paintings that show the Virgin Mary as being of average height. For example, in the painting 'The Virgin and Child with Saint Anne' by Leonardo da Vinci, Mary is shown to be of similar height to Saint Anne. This suggests that the artist believed her to be of average height. So, what can we conclude from all this? It is difficult to say for certain. However, it seems safe to say that the Virgin Mary was either tall or of average height.

Why did they break their legs on the cross?

The practice of breaking the legs of those who had been crucified died out by the fourth century, but for many centuries prior to that it was common for the Roman soldiers to do so. There are a few possible reasons for why they did this. The first reason is that it hastened death. Crucifixion was designed to be a slow and painful death, and one way to speed it up was to break the legs of the person who had been sentenced to it. This would prevent them from being able to push themselves up on their crossed feet in order to take a breath, and eventually they would suffocate. Another reason is that it was seen as a way to increase the shame and humiliation of the condemned person. The legs were usually the first to go when a person was being tortured, and so by breaking them the crucified person was being made to suffer even more. It is also possible that the soldiers simply enjoyed inflicting pain, and that they saw breaking the legs of those who had been crucified as a way to have some fun. Whatever the reason, it was a brutal practice that would have added to the already considerable suffering of those who were unfortunate enough to be sentenced to crucifixion.

What was the resurrection of Jesus?

The resurrection of Jesus is one of the most important events in the Christian faith. It is the belief that Jesus rose from the dead after being crucified, and that he is alive today. This event is central to the Christian message, and is what sets Christianity apart from other religions. The resurrection is mentioned in all four of the Gospels, and is attested to by many other ancient sources. Both Christian and non-Christian scholars agree that the event took place, and that it was of great importance. So what exactly happened on that day? The Gospels tell us that Jesus was crucified on a Friday, and that he was buried in a tomb. On the Sunday following his crucifixion, Jesus' tomb was found empty by his disciples. Jesus had risen from the dead, just as he had said he would. After his resurrection, Jesus appeared to many of his disciples over a period of 40 days. He also spoke to Paul, who would later become one of the most important figures in Christianity. After his time on earth, Jesus ascended into heaven, where he is alive today. The resurrection of Jesus is the most important event in history, because it proves that Jesus is who he said he was. He is the Son of God, and he has the power to forgive our sins. Because of his resurrection, we have hope for eternal life.

What verse is Jesus resurrection?

The resurrection of Jesus Christ is recorded in the final chapter of the Bible, Verse 24 says, "But on the first day of the week, at early dawn, they came to the tomb, bringing the spices which they had prepared." This is the only bible verse that explicitly states that Jesus was resurrected on the first day of the week, which we now call Easter. The first day of the week, or Easter, is a day of great importance to Christians. It is the day that Jesus rose from the dead, conquering death and sin. For Christians, Easter is a time of rejoicing, as they celebrate the risen Savior. The resurrection of Jesus is a central doctrine of Christianity. In fact, the Apostle Paul wrote in 1 Corinthians 15:17, "And if Christ has not been raised, your faith is futile and you are still in your sins." without the resurrection, Christianity would be a false religion. But because Jesus rose from the dead, we know that He is who He said He was- the Son of God. Easter is a time to celebrate the risen Savior. It is a time to remember that because Jesus conquered death, we can have hope for eternity. It is a time to reflect on the sacrifice that Jesus made for us, and to give thanks for His gift of eternal life.

Why is the resurrection of Jesus the most important event?

The death and resurrection of Jesus Christ is the most important event in human history. This is because, through His death and resurrection, Jesus conquered death and brought life and immortality to light. In doing so, He opened the way for all people to have a personal relationship with God. The resurrection of Jesus is the most important event because it affirms that He is who He said He is- the Son of God. His resurrection proves that His death was not simply a human death, but a sacrificial death that brought about our salvation. In His death, Jesus paid the price for our sin and His resurrection conquered death so that we may have new life in Him. The resurrection also affirms the truth of the gospel message. If Jesus had not risen from the dead, then His death would have been in vain and His message would have been proven false. But because He did rise from the dead, we know that He is who He said He is and that His message is true. The resurrection is also the most important event because it is the foundation of our hope. Because Jesus conquered death, we know that we, too, will one day be resurrected. This gives us hope in the midst of our trials and struggles, because we know that there is something better waiting for us. The resurrection is the most important event because it changed everything. Through His death and resurrection, Jesus brought about a new creation. He defeated death and brought life and immortality to light. He opened the way for all people to have a personal relationship with God. Because of the resurrection, we can have hope in the midst of our trials and know that there is something better waiting for us. The resurrection is the most important event because it changed everything.

Why is the resurrection so important?

The resurrection of Jesus Christ is the most important event in history. It is the cornerstone of Christianity and our hope for eternal life. Without the resurrection, Jesus would have just been a good man who died a cruel death. But because He rose from the dead, He proved that He is the Son of God and our Savior. The resurrection changed everything. It changed the way we view death, ourselves, and the world around us. Death is no longer the end, but a new beginning. Because Jesus rose from the dead, we know that we, too, will one day be raised from the dead. This gives us hope in the midst of hardship and sorrow. It gives us strength to face death with courage and confidence. The resurrection also changes the way we view ourselves. We are not defined by our sin or our mistakes. We are forgiven and loved by a God who sacrificed His own Son for us. We are new creations in Christ, and our lives have purpose and meaning. The resurrection also changes the way we view the world around us. This world is not our home, and we are not of this world. Our hope is in the one who conquered death, and we are called to live in light of that hope. The resurrection is the most important event in history because it changes everything. It changes the way we view death, ourselves, and the world around us. It gives us hope, strength, and purpose. It is the cornerstone of Christianity, and it is our hope for eternal life.

What is the true meaning of resurrection?

The celebration of Easter is a time of joy for Christians around the world as they remember and reflect on the resurrection of Jesus Christ. But what is the true meaning of resurrection? According to the Christian faith, resurrection is the belief that Jesus Christ rose from the dead on the third day after his crucifixion. This event is celebrated every year on Easter Sunday and is a fundamental belief of Christianity. The resurrection of Jesus Christ is significant as it shows that he has conquered death and that he is the Son of God. It is also a hope for Christians that they too will be resurrected after death. Resurrection is a central theme in the Bible and is one of the most important events in Christianity. In the Bible, Jesus Christ is raised from the dead by God the Father. This act shows that Jesus is the Son of God and has the power to defeat death. The resurrection of Jesus is also a hope for Christians. In 1 Corinthians 15:20-22 it says, "But now Christ has been raised from the dead, the first fruits of those who have fallen asleep. For since death came through a man, the resurrection of the dead comes also through a man. For as in Adam all die, so in Christ all will be made alive." This passage shows that just as Adam brought death into the world, Jesus brings life. This is significant as it shows that through Christ, we can have hope for eternal life. The resurrection of Jesus Christ is a powerful event that has changed the world. It is a reminder of God's love for us and His power to overcome death. It is also a hope for Christians that we too will one day be raised from the dead and have eternal life.

Although the origins of Easter are religious, the holiday has become more and more secularized over the years. For many people, Easter is now a time to spend with family, eat lots of chocolate, and maybe go on an Easter egg hunt. Whether you celebrate Easter for religious or secular reasons, or both, it's a time to enjoy the spring season and to celebrate new beginnings.

What is the promise of the resurrection?

According to the Bible, the resurrection is the promise of new life for Christians who have died. This new life is made possible by Jesus Christ, who conquered death when he rose from the dead. When Christ returns, he will complete the resurrection of all believers, bringing them back to new life. This is what is known as the 'first resurrection'. Christ will also raise up those who have not yet died, and they will be given new life too. This is the hope that Christians have – that through Christ, they will be given eternal life. This is not just a life after death, but a life that is full and abundant, and free from the pain and suffering of this world. Resurrection is a central theme of Christianity, and it is what sets us apart from other religions. It is the hope that gives us comfort in the midst of sorrow, and the assurance that no matter what happens in this life, we will be with Christ in the life to come.

What Bible says about resurrection?

The Bible is very clear that Jesus rose from the dead on the third day. This event is listed in all four of the Gospels. In addition, the Apostle Paul wrote about the resurrection in several of his Epistles. In 1 Corinthians 15, he even lists some of the people who saw Jesus after His resurrection. The resurrection is such an important event because it confirms that Jesus is who He said He was. He claimed to be the Son of God and the Savior of the world. His resurrection proves that He has the power to save us from our sins. It also proves that He has the power to overcome death. When Jesus died on the cross, He took the punishment for our sin. His death makes it possible for us to have a relationship with God. But, His resurrection is what gives us hope. It shows us that death is not the end. We will also be resurrected one day. The resurrection is a central doctrine of the Christian faith. Without it, our faith would be in vain. We would have no hope. But, because Jesus rose from the dead, we can have hope that death is not the end. We can have hope for eternal life.

What did Jesus do after his resurrection?

When Easter Sunday comes around, many people think of chocolate bunnies, Easter baskets, and Easter eggs. But what is the true meaning of Easter? And what did Jesus do after his resurrection? The word Easter actually comes from the word Eastre, which was the name of an Anglo-Saxon goddess. Her feast day was the Spring equinox, and it was a time for rebirth and fertility. The Christian holiday of Easter is a celebration of the resurrection of Jesus Christ. According to the Bible, after Jesus was crucified, he was buried in a tomb. On the third day, he rose from the dead. After his resurrection, Jesus appeared to many people. He appeared to his disciples, Mary Magdalene, and even to Saul (who later became Paul). Why did Jesus appear to all these people? Some say it was to prove that he was truly the Son of God. Others say it was to give hope to his followers. Whatever the reason, Jesus' appearances after his resurrection showed that he conquered death. Easter is a time to remember that Jesus is alive. He died on the cross for our sins, and he rose from the dead to give us new life. This is the message of Easter, and it is a message of hope for all who believe.

Why was Jesus resurrected on the third day?

The fourth day of Easter, also known as Easter Sunday, commemorates the resurrection of Jesus Christ. Christians believe that Jesus was crucified on the cross on Good Friday and was buried in a tomb. On the third day, known as Easter Sunday, Jesus rose from the dead. The resurrection of Jesus is one of the most important events in Christianity. The resurrection proves that Jesus is the Son of God and that he has the power to defeat death. The resurrection also gives hope to Christians that they will also be resurrected when they die. The Bible does not give a specific reason as to why Jesus was resurrected on the third day. Some Christians believe that the number three is symbolic of the Holy Trinity (the Father, the Son, and the Holy Spirit). Others believe that the third day represents the time that Jesus spend in the tomb, which was three days. Whatever the reason may be, the resurrection of Jesus is a significant event in Christianity. The resurrection gives Christians hope and a reason to celebrate.

Why is resurrection more important than crucifixion?

It is often said that Christianity is a religion of hope because of the resurrection of Jesus Christ. In fact, the resurrection is the central tenet of Christianity. But why is resurrection more important than crucifixion? The crucifixion of Jesus Christ was a horrific event. Jesus was tortured and then crucified. It was a cruel death. But Jesus did not stay dead. He was resurrected three days later. His resurrection conquering death forever. The resurrection is more important than the crucifixion because it shows that life is stronger than death. No matter how bad things might seem, no matter how dark and hopeless the world may appear, life will always triumph in the end. This is the message of the resurrection. The resurrection also shows that love is more powerful than hate. Jesus loved humanity so much that he was willing to die for us. His love conquered hate. And because of his love, we can have hope. The resurrection is the foundation of Christianity. It is what we base our hope on. It is what gives us comfort in the midst of sorrow and darkness. It is what gives us strength to go on. The reason resurrection is more important than crucifixion is because it gives us hope. Hope that no matter what happens in this life, we will be okay in the end. Hope that love will always triumph over hate. And hope that life will always be stronger than death.

How did resurrection save us?

The resurrection of Jesus Christ is the most important event in human history. It is the defining moment of Christianity. And it is the linchpin of our faith. The resurrection is so important because it is the event that shows that Jesus is who He said He is. He said He was the Son of God, sent to save us from our sins. And He said He would die and rise again. If Jesus didn't rise from the dead, then He was just a good man who had some interesting things to say. But if He did rise from the dead, then He is who He said He is, and His death and resurrection offer us the forgiveness of our sins and the hope of eternal life. The resurrection also shows us that death is not the end. Jesus conquered death. He showed that death cannot keep us from Him. And because He conquered death, we can have hope that death is not the end for us either. Because Jesus lives, we can live too. The resurrection is good news for us. It is the news that we are forgiven and that we have hope for the future. Because Jesus rose from the dead, we can have new life in Him.

Why did Jesus resurrect?

The resurrection of Jesus Christ is one of the most debated topics in history. Some say that Jesus never died on the cross and that His resurrection was nothing more than a legend. Others say that He died and was resurrected as a spirit. either way, the question remains: Why did Jesus resurrect? There are a number of theories as to why Jesus resurrected. One theory is that He did it to prove that He was the Son of God. By defeating death, Jesus showed that He had power over even the most powerful force in the universe. Another theory is that Jesus resurrected to show His followers that they, too, could defeat death. By rising from the dead, Jesus showed His followers that they, too, could have eternal life. Whatever the reason, there is no doubt that the resurrection of Jesus Christ is one of the most important events in history. Whether you believe that He did it to prove His divinity or to give hope to His followers, there is no denying that the resurrection of Jesus changed the world forever.

Easter is a holiday that is celebrated by many people around the world. It is a time to remember the sacrifice of Jesus Christ and to celebrate his resurrection. Easter is also a time for families to get together and to enjoy each other's company.

What are the two types of resurrection?

Most Christians believe in some form of resurrection, although there is debate over what exactly this entails. Some believe in a physical resurrection, in which the body is raised from the dead, while others believe in a spiritual resurrection, in which the soul is resurrected and the body remains in the ground. There are several biblical passages that mention resurrection, but the concept is also found in other religions. In Hinduism, for example, the concept of rebirth is central to their belief system. This idea of resurrection is different from the Christian concept, however, as it is not a one-time event but rather a continuous cycle. The concept of resurrection is a complex one, and there is still much debate over what it actually means. But for most Christians, the belief in resurrection is central to their faith, and it is an hope that gives them comfort in the face of death.

What was Jesus's full name?

First, let's start with the basics. Jesus's full name was Jeshua ben Joseph. Jeshua is the Hebrew name meaning "saves," while ben is the Hebrew word for "son of." Joseph is the name of Jesus's earthly father. But even that simple answer raises a lot of questions. For one, why did Jesus have a different name than His Father? And what's the significance of His full name? According to Jewish custom, a son was given his father's name. So if Joseph was Jesus's father, why wasn't He named Joseph? There are a couple of possible explanations. One is that Joseph wasn't really Jesus's father. The other is that, technically, He was not Joseph's firstborn son. The story of Jesus's birth tells us that He was born to a virgin named Mary. This means that Joseph was not His biological father. So, in that sense, His name wasn't Joseph. However, Joseph was still His legal father. In Jewish culture, the legal father was the one who was married to the child's mother. So even though Joseph wasn't Jesus's biological father, he was still His father in the eyes of the law. But there's another wrinkle to this story. Joseph was not Jesus's firstborn son. Before Jesus was born, Mary was betrothed to Joseph. This was more than just an engagement; it was a binding legal contract. However, before the contract was finalized, Mary became pregnant with Jesus. This meant that, in the eyes of the law, Joseph was not really Jesus' father. So, technically, Jesus's full name should have been Jeshua ben Joseph ben David, meaning "saves, son of Joseph, son of David." But why was His name Jeshua instead of Joseph? There are a few possible explanations. One is that, since Joseph was not really His father, it would have been improper to give Him his father's name. Another explanation is that, since Joseph was already a common name, it would have been confusing to have two people with the same name. So, instead of giving Him the name Joseph, they chose the name Jeshua, which was a common name at the time. Interestingly, the name Jeshua was not originally a Hebrew name. It was actually a Babylonian name that the Jews adopted after they were exiled to Babylon. So, in a way, the name Jeshua was a symbol of hope for the Jews. It was a reminder that, even though they were in exile

What is the gift of resurrection?

Resurrection is the gift of new life. It is the hope that we have in Christ that death is not the end, but rather the beginning of eternal life with Him. Christ's resurrection assures us that our sins are forgiven and that we will one day be reunited with our loved ones who have gone before us. It is the hope that gives us strength to face our own death with confidence, knowing that we too will one day be raised up to new life. Resurrection is a powerful gift that gives new meaning to our lives. It is a reminder that no matter what trials and tribulations we face in this life, there is always hope. Christ's resurrection reminds us that we are never alone, and that God is always with us. Even in the darkest of times, we can take comfort in knowing that Christ has overcoming death, and that He will one day return to take us home to be with Him for eternity.

What are the last words of Jesus?

What are the last words of Jesus? Some say that Jesus' final words were "it is finished," while others believe that his last words were "father, into your hands I commend my spirit." No one can know for sure what Jesus' last words were, but we do know that they were powerful and full of meaning. When Jesus spoke his final words, he had just completed the work of salvation. He had given his life as a sacrifice for our sins, and he had conquered death. His work was finished, and he had accomplished everything he had set out to do. But even though his work was done, he still had more to say. Jesus' last words were a prayer to his father. He asked that his spirit be commended into his father's hands. This was a sign of his complete trust and submission to God. Even in his dying moments, Jesus was still focused on God and his will. These last words of Jesus show us his complete trust in God, even in the face of death. They also remind us that we should always be focused on God and his will for our lives. As we strive to follow Jesus, we should keep these last words in mind and let them guide our lives.

What did Jesus do in the 40 days between resurrection and ascension?

It is said that Jesus spent forty days between His resurrection and ascension. But what did He do during that time? The Bible tells us that He spent time with His disciples, teaching them and preparing them for the work that lay ahead. He also appeared to many people, both believers and unbelievers alike. His appearances were often sudden and unexpected, and He would often vanish just as quickly. On one occasion, Jesus took Peter, James and John up a mountain with Him. There, He was transfigured before them, His face shining like the sun and His clothes becoming as white as the light. This was a glimpse of His glory, something that His disciples would have to remember when He was gone. Another time, Jesus took some bread and fish and fed a huge crowd of people. When they had all eaten their fill, He instructed His disciples to gather up the leftover food. Miraculously, there was enough to feed them all and there were even some baskets left over. Throughout these forty days, Jesus continued to teach and show His love for His people. He healed the sick, He comforted the sorrowful and He showed His disciples the way that they should go. He also promised that He would be with them always, even to the end of the age. Then, on the fortieth day, Jesus ascended into heaven. He left His disciples with a final instruction to go out into the world and spread the Good News. And He promised that He would one day return. So what did Jesus do during the forty days between His resurrection and ascension? He spent time with His disciples, He taught them, He healed the sick, He fed the hungry and He promised to always be with them.

How long was Jesus dead before he came back to life?

How long was Jesus dead before he came back to life? This is a question that has puzzled historians, religious scholars, and ordinary people for centuries. There is no clear answer in the Bible, and scholars have offered a range of estimates based on their interpretation of the text. Some believe that Jesus was dead for only a few hours before he was resurrected. This view is based on the fact that the Jewish day began at sundown, so Jesus would have been crucified on Friday afternoon and resurrected sometime on Saturday. Others believe that Jesus was dead for three days and nights, as he himself predicted. This view is based on a close reading of the Gospel accounts, which indicate that Jesus was crucified on Friday and resurrected on Sunday. Still others believe that Jesus was dead for longer than three days. This view is based on the fact that it takes time for a body to decompose, and Jesus' body would not have had time to decompose if he was only dead for three days. Whatever the case may be, it is clear that Jesus' resurrection was a miraculous event that goes against the laws of nature. And for Christians, it is a sign that Jesus is who he said he was – the Son of God.

What did Jesus do 3 days after he was crucified?

When Jesus died on the cross, he was buried in a tomb. Three days later, he rose from the dead. This is called the Resurrection. After the Resurrection, Jesus spent 40 days on earth talking with his disciples and teaching them. Then he ascended into heaven.

There are many different traditions and activities associated with Easter, but the underlying reason for celebrating is the same – to rejoice in the resurrection of Jesus Christ. Whether you choose to spend Easter Sunday in church, with family, or participating in fun activities, the holiday is a time to reflect on the hope and new life that comes with Christ's sacrifice.

Where did Jesus go after his death?

The Easter story is one of the most important in Christianity. It tells of Jesus' death and resurrection, which Christians believe happened over 2,000 years ago. But what happened to Jesus after his death? According to the Bible, Jesus was crucified and died on the cross. His body was then placed in a tomb and he was buried. Three days later, Jesus rose from the dead and appeared to his disciples. After appearing to them, he ascended into heaven. So, what happened to Jesus after his death? Christians believe that he rose from the dead and ascended into heaven.

Why is Jesus death so important?

The death of Jesus Christ is the most important event in human history. Without the death and resurrection of Jesus, there would be no Christianity. Christianity is founded on the belief that Jesus died for our sins and rose again. If Jesus had not died, then he would not have been able to save us from our sins. The death of Jesus Christ is so important because it is the Event that defeating sin and death. Sin and death have been our enemies since the fall of man. They have caused all the suffering and hurt in the world. But Jesus came and he conquered sin and death by dying on the cross. His death means that we no longer have to be controlled by our sin. We can now be free from the bondage of sin. The resurrection of Jesus is also key to Christianity. If Jesus had not risen from the dead, then his death would have just been another death. But because he rose from the dead, we know that his death was not in vain. He conquered death, and because of that we can have hope. We know that our own death is not the end. We will also rise from the dead, and we will live with Jesus forever. The death and resurrection of Jesus Christ is the most important event in human history because it is the event that gives us hope. Hope for a forgiven life, hope for a future with Jesus, and hope for eternity. Thank you Jesus for dying for us. Thank you for giving us hope.

What did Jesus do 40 days before his crucifixion?

When Jesus was crucified, he had already been through a lot. He had been betrayed by one of his closest friends, been put on trial, and had been killed. But what did he do in the 40 days leading up to his crucifixion? First, let's look at what he did during the 40 days after his resurrection. After he rose from the dead, he appeared to his disciples and then ascended into heaven. But before that, he spent 40 days on earth, teaching and preaching. And what did he teach about? One of the things he taught about was the kingdom of God. He told his disciples that the kingdom of God was coming soon. He also taught them about how to pray and how to live their lives according to God's will. In the 40 days before his crucifixion, Jesus also spent time preparing his disciples for what was to come. He knew that they would soon be without him, and so he wanted to make sure that they knew what to do. He taught them about the importance of evangelism and how to spread the gospel. He also warned them about the dangers of false teachers and how to avoid them. Jesus knew that his time on earth was coming to an end, and so he spent his last days preparing his disciples for the work that they would need to do after he was gone. He taught them about the kingdom of God and how to live their lives according to God's will. And he prepared them for the task of evangelism that would be their mission after he was gone.

What are the blessings of the resurrection?

The resurrection of Jesus Christ is the most important event in history. It is the cornerstone of the Christian faith. without it, our faith would be in vain. The resurrection proves that Jesus is who He said He is- the Son of God. He conquered death, hell, and the grave. He did this so that we could have eternal life. The resurrection also gives us hope. We know that because Jesus rose from the dead, we can have hope that one day we will too. death is not the end. There is more to our story than what meets the eye. The resurrection is a reminder that we are never alone. Jesus is with us always. He knows what we are going through because He went through it Himself. He is a sympathetic high priest who can help us in our time of need. The resurrection is also a call to action. Because Jesus rose from the dead, we are called to share the good news with others. We are called to love our neighbor, no matter how difficult they may be to love. All of these blessings and more are available to us because of the resurrection. It is the most important event in history because it changed everything.

How many people did Jesus appear to after his resurrection?

How many people did Jesus appear to after resurrection? This is a question that has long puzzled scholars and believers alike. The Bible gives us some clues, but no definitive answer. One of the most famous appearances is, of course, the one to Mary Magdalene. We are told that she went to the tomb early on the morning of the resurrection, and found it empty. She then saw Jesus, who spoke to her and told her to go and tell the others that he had risen from the dead. Another appearance that is often mentioned is the one to the disciples on the road to Emmaus. Here, two of Jesus' followers are walking along, discussing the recent events in Jerusalem, when Jesus himself appears and joins in their conversation. They only realise who he is when he breaks bread with them at the end of the meal. The Bible also tells us that Jesus appeared to his disciples several times over a period of forty days, before he ascended into heaven. On one occasion, he even ate with them to prove that he was really alive and not just a ghost. So, we know that Jesus appeared to at least three different groups of people: his disciples, the Emmaus disciples and Mary Magdalene. But the Bible doesn't give us a definite number for how many individuals this amounted to. It's possible that there were other appearances that we don't know about. Whatever the case may be, it is certain that Jesus' resurrection was a real event, witnessed by many people. And it is because of this that we have hope that we too will one day be raised from the dead, to live with him forever.

Who raised Jesus from the dead?

The resurrection of Jesus Christ is one of the most important events in human history. Jesus was crucified on a cross and died as a result of his crucifixion. His body was placed in a tomb and he was buried. On the third day, Jesus rose from the dead. He appeared to his disciples and many others over a period of forty days. After his ascension into heaven, Jesus left his disciples with the command to spread the good news of the gospel to all people. The resurrection of Jesus Christ is a historical fact. It is an event that is attested to by multiple eyewitnesses. The accounts of the resurrection are found in the four Gospels of the Bible. These accounts are reliable and trustworthy. The resurrection of Jesus is a central doctrine of Christianity. Christians believe that Jesus was raised from the dead by the power of God. The resurrection of Jesus Christ is a miracle. Jesus was raised from the dead by the power of the Holy Spirit. His resurrection proves that he is the Son of God. The resurrection also proves that death has been defeated. Jesus defeated death by his resurrection. Those who believe in him will also be raised from the dead. The resurrection of Jesus Christ is good news. It is the best news ever. Jesus is alive and he is coming back again. He is the only way to eternal life. When we trust in him, we will be forgiven of our sins and we will have eternal life.

Who was the first person to rise from the dead in the Bible?

The first person in the Bible to rise from the dead is Lazarus. Lazarus was the brother of Mary and Martha and lived in Bethany. Lazarus became ill and died. When Martha and Mary went to Jesus and told him that Lazarus had died, Jesus wept. Then, Jesus went to Bethany and raised Lazarus from the dead. This event is significant because it shows that Jesus has the power over death. Lazarus had been dead for four days, but Jesus was able to bring him back to life. This miracle demonstrated that Jesus has the authority to give life and to take it away. The raising of Lazarus also foreshadowed Jesus' own resurrection. Just as Lazarus was raised from the dead, so Jesus would be raised from the dead. On the third day after his crucifixion, Jesus rose from the dead, defeating death once and for all. Because of Jesus' resurrection, we also have the hope of resurrection. When we die, we will not stay dead, but will be raised to new life, just like Lazarus. This is the hope that we have because of Jesus Christ.

There are many different traditions that are celebrated during Easter, but the holiday always signifies new beginnings. Whether it is springtime, new life, or a fresh start, Easter is a time to reflect on the blessings in our lives. We can all use a little reminder to be grateful for what we have, and Easter is the perfect time for that.

Where in the Bible does it say the dead will rise first?

The Bible teaches that the dead will rise first at the last trumpet. This is found in 1 Corinthians 15:52. "For the trumpet will sound, and the dead will be raised incorruptible, and we shall be changed." This is also backed up by Revelation 20:4-6 which says, "And I saw thrones, and they sat on them, and judgment was committed to them. Then I saw the souls of those who had been beheaded for their witness to Jesus and for the word of God, who had not worshiped the beast or his image, and had not received his mark on their foreheads or on their hands. And they lived and reigned with Christ for a thousand years. But the rest of the dead did not live again until the thousand years were finished. This is the first resurrection." So we can see that the Bible clearly teaches that the dead will rise first, and then those who are alive will be changed. This will happen at the last trumpet.

What is Jesus's actual birthday?

One of the most well-known and celebrated holidays in Christianity is Easter, which celebrates the resurrection of Jesus Christ. Though the holiday always falls on a Sunday, the date of Easter varies from year to year. This is because Easter is a moveable feast, meaning that its date is not based on the Gregorian or Julian calendar, but rather the lunar one. The first full moon of spring is used to calculate the holiday, as well as the Jewish Passover. Because of this, some years Easter can fall as early as March 22 or as late as April 25. In 325 AD, the first Council of Nicaea was convened in order to establish an official date for Easter. They decided that it should be held on the first Sunday after the first full moon occurring on or after the vernal equinox. This means that, in theory, Easter could be as early as March 22 or as late as April 25. Interestingly, the holiday was not always celebrated on a Sunday. In fact, it was not until after the resurrection of Christ that the day of the week was changed. This was likely done in order to avoid confusion with Jewish celebrations and to make the holiday more accessible to pagans. So, what is the actual birthday of Jesus Christ? Unfortunately, because the holiday is based on the lunar calendar, we cannot know for certain. However, many scholars believe that Christ was most likely born in early September, based on the fact that shepherds were tending to their flocks in the fields at night. Easter is a holiday with a long and rich history, full of both religious and cultural significance. Though we may not know the exact date of Jesus's birth, the holiday provides us with a time to reflect on his life, death, and resurrection, and to celebrate the hope that he brings to us all.

What are the 3 gifts to Jesus?

What are the 3 gifts to Jesus? easter is a holiday that celebrates the resurrection of Jesus Christ. It is also a time when many people give gifts to friends and loved ones. But what if you want to give a gift to Jesus? What are the best gifts to give him? The first gift you could give Jesus is the gift of your time. Spend time with him in prayer and reflect on all that he has done for you. Give thanks for his blessings and ask for his guidance in your life. The second gift you could give Jesus is the gift of your talent. Use the gifts and talents that he has given you to make the world a better place. Help others in his name and spread his message of love and forgiveness. The third gift you could give Jesus is the gift of your treasure. Give generously to those in need and to organizations that help others. May your gifts be a blessing to others and bring glory to Jesus Christ.

What are the 3 God given gifts?

There are three gifts that God has given to us: love, hope, and faith. These gifts are what sustain us through difficult times and help us to overcome challenges. God's love is always there for us, no matter what we've done or where we are in life. His love is unconditional and doesn't waver. This love gives us hope that we are never alone and that we can always rely on Him. Faith is another one of God's gifts to us. It is what allows us to believe in His existence and trust in His plan for us. Faith gives us strength when we are facing trials and helps us to see the light at the end of the tunnel. Lastly, hope is a gift from God that gives us a sense of peace and joy. It is the knowledge that no matter what happens in this life, we will ultimately be okay. Hope gives us the strength to keep going when times are tough and to believe that better days are ahead. These three gifts from God are what make life worth living. They sustain us through the tough times and help us to appreciate the good times. We should never take them for granted, but instead be thankful for all that God has given us.

Does the Bible say Jesus was crucified?

The Bible says very little about the crucifixion of Jesus. The gospels of Matthew, Mark, and Luke each mention the crucifixion in a single sentence; the gospel of John does not mention it at all. The book of Acts, written later, also mentions the crucifixion in a single sentence. None of the gospel writers give any details about the crucifixion, such as who was present or what was said. The lack of detail in the Bible about the crucifixion raises questions for some people. If the crucifixion was such an important event in the life of Jesus, why isn't there more information about it in the Bible? There are a few possible explanations for the lack of detail about the crucifixion in the Bible. First, it is possible that the early Christians were not concerned with providing a detailed account of the event. The focus of the gospels is on the resurrection of Jesus, not on his death. Second, the gospel writers may have chosen not to include more information about the crucifixion because they did not want to offend readers who were not familiar with the details of crucifixion. Crucifixion was a method of execution that was reserved for the worst criminals. It was a slow and painful death, and it was considered to be very humiliating. The early Christians were likely to have been familiar with crucifixion, but many of their non-Christian contemporaries would not have been. The lack of detail about the crucifixion in the Bible should not be viewed as a lack of important. The crucifixion was a vital part of God's plan for salvation. Jesus died on the cross so that we could be forgiven for our sins. His death conquered death itself, and because of Jesus we can have eternal life.

What was Jesus crucified for?

When Jesus was crucified, there was a sign that was placed above his head that said, "Jesus of Nazareth, the King of the Jews." Why was this? Was he really a king? According to the Gospels, Jesus was arrested and brought before the Sanhedrin, accused of claiming to be King of the Jews. The Jewish leaders were not expecting him to deny it, but instead wanted him to confirm the claim so they could have a basis to accuse him of blasphemy, which was punishable by death under Jewish law. Interestingly, the Gospel of Mark says that when Jesus was brought before Pilate, the governor asked him if he was the King of the Jews and Jesus replied, "You say that I am." Luke's account is similar, but with a subtle difference - instead of saying "You say that I am", Jesus says, "You say correctly that I am." So what did Jesus mean? Was he in fact claiming to be a earthly king, as his accusers claimed? The answer may lie in the fact that, throughout the Gospels, Jesus consistently speaks of his kingdom as being "not of this world." In John 18:36, for example, he tells Pilate, "My kingdom is not from this world. If my kingdom were from this world, my servants would be fighting." It's possible that when Jesus said "You say correctly that I am," he was acknowledging that, in a sense, he was a king - but not an earthly one. He was the King of a spiritual kingdom that was not bound by earthly limitations. Of course, we can't know for sure what Jesus meant. But it's interesting to think about what his answer might have meant in the context of his larger message.

What chapter in the Bible does Jesus get crucified?

In the Bible, Jesus Christ is crucified in chapter 27 of the Gospel of Matthew, chapter 27 of the Gospel of Mark, and chapter 23 of the Gospel of Luke. All three of these chapters are part of the Passion narrative, which tells the story of Jesus' arrest, trial, crucifixion, and resurrection. The Passion narrative is one of the most well-known and well-loved stories in the Bible. It is a story of hope and redemption, in which Jesus gives his life for the forgiveness of our sins. This story has been a source of inspiration and comfort for centuries, and it continues to be one of the most popular stories in the Bible.

Easter is a joyful time of year when Christians celebrate the resurrection of Jesus Christ. It is a time for hope, new beginnings, and celebrating the life that Jesus promised us. Easter is a special time to come together with family and friends, and to Reflect on the meaning of the holiday.

Where was Jesus been crucified?

The Bible does not give a specific answer as to where Jesus was crucified. It simply says that it was outside the city walls of Jerusalem. This is consistent with other ancient accounts of crucifixion, which typically took place outside city walls. Scholars have proposed several possible locations for the crucifixion site, but the precise location remains unknown. Some believe that Jesus was crucified at a place called Golgotha, which means "the place of the skull". This name may have come from the shape of the hill on which it was located, or it may have been because crucifixions often took place there. It is also possible that the name was given due to the large number of crucifixions that took place there. Another possible location for the crucifixion is a place called Gordon's Calvary. This is a hill located just outside the city walls of Jerusalem, and it matches the description of Golgotha in some ancient texts. It is also the site of a large number of tombs, which could explain the name "place of the skull". Ultimately, the precise location of the crucifixion site is unknown. However, it is most likely that Jesus was crucified outside the city walls of Jerusalem, at a place called Golgotha or Gordon's Calvary.

What did Jesus say to God when he was crucified?

When Jesus was crucified, he said a lot of things to God. He asked God to forgive the people who were crucifying him, and he also asked God to help him bear the pain of the crucifixion. He also said that he was willing to obey God's will, even if it meant dying on the cross. Lastly, he asked God to ascend him to heaven.

Did Jesus bleed when he was crucified?

Did Jesus bleed when he was crucified? It is a question that has long puzzled historians, and one that has been the subject of intense debate. Some say that the answer is yes, while others argue that the evidence suggests otherwise. So what is the truth? It is certainly true that the Crucifixion was a brutal and bloody affair. The Roman historian Tacitus, writing in the first century, described it as "a cruel and disgusting death". And the Bible tells us that Jesus was crucified along with two thieves. So it is possible that Jesus did bleed when he was crucified. However, there is also evidence to suggest that he did not. For one thing, the Bible says that Jesus was crucified at the third hour (9am) and died at the ninth hour (3pm). This would suggest that he died relatively quickly, which would be unlikely if he had been bleeding heavily. There is also the fact that, in John's Gospel, Jesus is described as having his linen garments removed before he is crucified. This would not have been necessary if he had been covered in blood. So what is the truth? Did Jesus bleed when he was crucified? We may never know for certain. But whatever the answer, the fact remains that the Crucifixion was a horrific event, and one that would have been extremely painful and bloody.

Why did Jesus allow himself to be crucified?

It is difficult to say definitively why Jesus allowed himself to be crucified. Perhaps he knew that it was his fate and that it was necessary for him to die in order to save humanity from its sins. Or, maybe he believed that his death would send a powerful message about the power of love and sacrifice. Either way, Jesus' decision to go through with his crucifixion was no doubt a courageous one. In the days leading up to his crucifixion, Jesus knew that he was going to die. He could have run away or hidden, but instead he chose to stand up to his accusers. He could have fought back against the Roman soldiers who were going to nail him to the cross, but instead he submitted to their authority. In doing so, Jesus showed incredible strength and courage. Some people believe that Jesus allowed himself to be crucified because he loved humanity and wanted to save us from our sins. By dying on the cross, Jesus took on the weight of all our sin and suffering. In doing so, he sacrificed himself for the greater good. His act of selfless love is one of the things that makes him such an inspirational figure. Others believe that Jesus' death was a powerful statement about the unjust treatment of people who challenge the status quo. Jesus was a radical thinker who preached love and compassion. He challenged the authorities of his day and they responded by killing him. In dying, Jesus showed that love is more powerful than hatred and that truth will always triumph in the end. Whatever the reason, Jesus' decision to allow himself to be crucified was a brave and courageous one. He could have chosen an easier path, but instead he chose the path of love and sacrifice. In doing so, he changed the course of history and inspired billions of people.

What three things happened when Jesus was crucified?

When Jesus was crucified, three things happened. First, he was betrayed by Judas Iscariot. Second, he was tried and convicted by Pontius Pilate. Third, he was crucified by the Roman soldiers. When Judas Iscariot betrayed Jesus, he kiss him on the cheek in front of the soldiers. This was a signal to the soldiers that this was the man they were looking for. Then, Jesus was tried by Pontius Pilate. Pilate found no evidence that Jesus had committed any crime, but the people were demanding that Jesus be crucified. So, Pilate washed his hands of the whole situation and had Jesus crucified. The Roman soldiers took Jesus to a hill called Golgotha and crucified him. They nailed his hands and feet to the cross and then raised him up so that everyone could see him. Jesus hung on the cross for six hours before he died.

What did Jesus do after he was crucified?

The Bible tells us that after Jesus was crucified, he was buried in a tomb. On the third day, he rose from the dead and appeared to his disciples. After that, he ascended into heaven. What did Jesus do after he was resurrected? The Bible doesn't give us a lot of details, but we know that he appeared to his disciples and many other people over a period of 40 days. During that time, he taught them about the kingdom of God. He also prepared them for his ascension into heaven. Jesus gave his disciples a special mission: to spread the good news about God's love and forgiveness to the whole world. He promised that he would be with them always, even when they were facing difficult times. When Jesus ascended into heaven, he didn't leave his disciples alone. He sent them the Holy Spirit to guide and comfort them. And he promised to come back again someday. We don't know exactly what happened to Jesus after he was resurrected, but we do know that he is alive and is with us always.

Where did Jesus do after he died?

It is a common misconception that Jesus simply vanished after his crucifixion – that he died and his body was never found. In actuality, there are a number of different accounts of Jesus' whereabouts in the hours and days after his death. The first account comes from the Bible itself. The Gospel of Matthew says that after Jesus died, he was buried in a tomb by Joseph of Arimathea. After Jesus' body was laid in the tomb, a large stone was rolled in front of the entrance to seal it shut. On the third day, Jesus rose from the dead and his tomb was found empty. A second account of Jesus' post-mortem whereabouts comes from the Muslim tradition. According to the Quran, Jesus was not killed on the cross but was raised up to heaven by God. Muslims believe that Jesus will return to earth before the Day of Judgment. A third account comes from the ancient Jewish historian, Josephus. Josephus' account is unique in that he was not a Christian or a Muslim, but he still wrote about Jesus. Josephus says that after Jesus was crucified, his body was taken down from the cross and given to his family for burial. So what really happened to Jesus after he died? The truth is, we don't know for sure. What we do know is that Jesus' followers believed that he rose from the dead and that he is alive today.

Easter is a religious holiday that celebrates the resurrection of Jesus Christ. It is observed by Christians all over the world and is one of the most important holidays in the Christian calendar. Easter is a time of hope and renewal, and is a reminder of the power of faith.

Who stole the true cross?

In the Christian tradition, the True Cross is the physical remnant of the cross upon which Jesus was crucified. For centuries, Christian pilgrims have journeyed to Jerusalem in order to view the relic and venerate it. In recent years, however, there has been much debate surrounding the authenticity of the True Cross. Some argue that it was stolen by Crusaders during the 11th century, while others claim that it was taken by the Persians during the 7th century. The True Cross first came into the possession of Emperor Constantine in the 4th century. According to tradition, Constantine's mother, Helena, found the True Cross while on a pilgrimage to Jerusalem. She is said to have been directed to the location by a vision of a bright light. After uncovering the relic, Helena brought it back to Constantinople, where it was placed in the Church of the Holy Sepulchre. The True Cross remained in Constantinople for centuries, until the city was sacked by the Crusaders in 1204. During the confusion of the sack, the True Cross was stolen and taken to Venice, where it was put on display in the Church of San Marco. The Venetians eventually sold the relic to the Knights Templars, who brought it to Paris. The True Cross remained in Paris for over 200 years, until it was stolen by the Persians during the Siege of Paris in 1794. The Persians took the relic to Ctesiphon, where it was placed in the Church of the Cross. The True Cross remained in Ctesiphon until the city was captured by the Arabs in 637. The current whereabouts of the True Cross are unknown. It is possible that it was destroyed during the Muslim conquest of Ctesiphon, or that it was taken back to Jerusalem by the Crusaders. There is also a possibility that the True Cross is still in Ctesiphon, hidden away in a secret location. Whatever the case may be, the True Cross is one of the most elusive relics in history, and its true location may never be known.

What did Jesus say about his death?

There is a lot of debate surrounding the exact words that Jesus spoke surrounding his death, but there are some common themes that are generally agreed upon. For example, Jesus spoke about how his death would be a sacrifice for the sins of others, and how he would be resurrected after three days. It is clear that Jesus knew his death was coming, and he was not afraid of it. He was willing to lay down his life for the greater good, and he had full trust in his father's plan. Jesus spoke about how his death would bring new life to others, and how it would be a victory over evil. These are just a few of the things that Jesus said about his death. It is clear that he had a strong understanding of what was going to happen, and he was at peace with it. He was willing to sacrifice himself for the sake of others, and he knew that his death would not be the end.

What was Jesus last word before he died?

As Jesus was dying on the cross, he uttered a final phrase: "Father, into your hands I commit my spirit." This was a quote from Psalm 31:5, which read, "Into your hands I commit my spirit; deliver me, Lord, my faithful God." By uttering these words, Jesus was expressing his trust in God and his hope for deliverance. He was also acknowledging that his life was coming to an end. These last words of Jesus are significant for a number of reasons. First, they show us that Jesus was a devout Jew who was well-versed in the scriptures. He knew that the psalmist had committed his spirit to God and had asked for deliverance. In the same way, Jesus was committing his spirit to God and asking for deliverance. Second, these words show us that Jesus was a man of great faith. He trusted that God would receive his spirit and that he would be delivered from his suffering. Third, these words reveal the intimacy of Jesus' relationship with God. He saw God as his father and entrusted his spirit into His care. Fourth, these words give us hope. In Jesus' time of greatest trial, he looked to God and found hope. As we face our own trials, we can look to Jesus and find hope in Him. Fifth, these words remind us that Jesus is Lord. He is the one who has ultimate authority over our lives. When we commit our lives to Him, we are putting our trust in the one who is ultimately in control. These last words of Jesus offer us comfort, hope, and direction in our own lives. As we face trials and challenges, we can turn to Jesus and find strength in His example. We can also trust that He is in control and that He will ultimately triumph over all evil.

What was Jesus last words at death?

What were Jesus' last words at death? There is much debate over what Jesus' final words were before he died. Some say that he said, "Father, forgive them, for they know not what they do." Others believe that his last words were, "It is finished." Whatever Jesus' final words were, we can be certain that they were filled with love, compassion, and forgiveness. In his last moments, Jesus was thinking of others and praying for their forgiveness. This shows us the true nature of Jesus - a man who was full of love, even for those who were persecuted him. Jesus' final words are a reminder to us that we should always forgive others, no matter how difficult it may be. We should strive to show the same compassion and love that Jesus showed in his final moments. By doing so, we can honor his memory and reflect the light of Christ to the world.

How painful is crucifixion?

Crucifixion is one of the most painful methods of execution ever devised. The victim is literally nailed to a cross and left to hang there until they die. The weight of their body, combined with the position of their arms and legs, makes it impossible for them to move. As the hours or days go by, their body starts to shut down. They will experience thirst, hunger, and eventually, death. Although the exact details of how crucifixion was carried out vary from historical source to historical source, we do know that it was an incredibly painful way to die. The victim would be nailed or tied to a cross and left to hang there until they died. Their body weight, combined with the position of their arms and legs, would make it impossible for them to move. This would cause them to experience thirst, hunger, and eventually, death. We also know that crucifixion was not always quick. In some cases, the victim would be left to hang on the cross for days before finally succumbing to their injuries. This would only add to the pain and suffering they experienced. So, to answer the question, crucifixion is extremely painful. It is a slow and torturous way to die. There is no way to escape the pain, as the victim is completely immobilized. If you find yourself in a situation where you might be crucified, know that it will be one of the most painful things you could ever experience.

Why did they break the legs of the crucified?

The practice of breaking the legs of crucified victims was called crurifragium, and was done to hasten death. The legs were broken with an iron club or some other blunt instrument. This ensured that the person could no longer push themselves up to take a breath, and would eventually suffocate. There are several reasons why the Romans might have implemented this practice. First, it was seen as a mercy. If the victim died quickly, they would not have to suffer the prolonged agony of crucifixion. Second, it helped to deter would-be criminals. The thought of being crucified was bad enough, but the added horror of having one's legs broken would surely discourage anyone from committing a crime. Finally, it was a way to control the victim. By breaking their legs, the Romans could ensure that the victim could not escape. This was especially useful in times of uprising or rebellion, when it was necessary to quickly quell any dissent. While the practice of breaking the legs of crucified victims may seem cruel, it served a purpose in the Roman Empire. By hastening death, deterring crime, and controlling the victim, crurifragium was a tool that the Romans used to maintain order and keep the peace.

How long did Jesus stay on the cross after he died?

The Bible does not give a definite answer as to how long Jesus stayed on the cross after he died. Theories abound, but without clear Scriptural evidence, it is impossible to say for certain. Some believe that Jesus died relatively quickly on the cross. A quick death would have been more humane, and it is possible that the soldiers hastened his death in order to get the executions over with. Others believe that Jesus died more slowly and that his body was left on the cross for some time after his death. This was not an uncommon practice in crucifixion, as it ensured that the criminal was truly dead and would not come back to life. Whatever the case, it is certain that Jesus died on the cross and that his body was taken down and buried soon after. His death and resurrection are central to Christian faith, and we can be confident that he died and rose again, regardless of the details of his crucifixion.

Overall, Easter is a happy and exciting holiday. It is a time for families to get together, celebrate, and enjoy each other's company. Children look forward to receiving Easter baskets filled with goodies, and everyone enjoys participating in Easter egg hunts. Whether you are religious or not, Easter is a fun-filled holiday that is enjoyed by all.

Who killed Jesus on the cross and why?

The question of who killed Jesus on the cross has been debated for centuries. There are many theories and no definitive answer. Some say that the Romans killed Jesus because he was a political threat. Others say that the Jews killed Jesus because he was a religious threat. There is evidence to support both theories. The Roman theory is based on the fact that the Romans were in charge of crucifixions. They were the ones who had the power to sentence someone to death by crucifixion. Crucifixion was a form of execution that was reserved for the worst criminals. The fact that Jesus was crucified shows that the Romans considered him to be a serious criminal. The Jewish theory is based on the fact that the Jews were the ones who accused Jesus of blasphemy. Blasphemy was a serious crime in Jewish law. The fact that the Jews accused Jesus of blasphemy shows that they considered him to be a serious threat to their religion. both the Roman and Jewish theories have evidence to support them. There is no definitive answer to the question of who killed Jesus on the cross.

Who was the first person to go to heaven alive?

The first person to go to heaven alive was Jesus Christ. He was crucified on the cross and died for our sins. But on the third day he rose from the dead and ascended into heaven. Jesus is the only one who has ever been to heaven while alive. Everyone else who has gone to heaven has done so after they died. Jesus is the only one who has ever been to heaven while alive. Everyone else who has gone to heaven has done so after they died. This is because when Jesus died, he conquered death. He rose from the dead and showed us that death no longer has any power over us. Because of this, we can have hope that when we die, we will also go to heaven. Jesus is the only one who has ever been to heaven while alive. Everyone else who has gone to heaven has done so after they died. This is because when Jesus died, he conquered death. He rose from the dead and showed us that death no longer has any power over us. Because of this, we can have hope that when we die, we will also go to heaven. Jesus is the only one who has ever been to heaven while alive. Everyone else who has gone to heaven has done so after they died. This is because when Jesus died, he conquered death. He rose from the dead and showed us that death no longer has any power over us. Because of this, we can have hope that when we die, we will also go to heaven.

What does the H stand for in Jesus name?

What does the H stand for in Jesus name? The H in Jesus' name may represent the Hebrew letter Chet, which is the first letter of the Hebrew word meaning "Life". In the New Testament, Jesus is given the title "the incarnation of the eternal Logos". The H might also represent the first letter of the Greek word for "Lord", which is Ἄνθρωπος (anthropos).

What language did Adam and Eve speak?

When it comes to the question of what language Adam and Eve spoke, there are a few different schools of thought. Many people believe that Adam and Eve spoke Hebrew, as that is the language of the Bible. Others believe that they spoke a form of Aramaic, as that was the language of Jesus. Still others believe that they spoke a language that is now lost to history. The truth is, we don't really know what language Adam and Eve spoke. The Bible doesn't give us a clear answer, and there is no other historical record that can tell us for sure. So, we can only speculate. Some people believe that Adam and Eve spoke Hebrew because the Bible is written in that language. Hebrew is also the language of the Jews, who are the descendants of Abraham, who was a contemporary of Moses (who wrote the first five books of the Bible). Others believe that Aramaic is a more likely choice for the language of Adam and Eve. Aramaic was the language of Jesus, and it was also the lingua franca of the Middle East during the time of the Roman Empire. Still, others believe that the language of Adam and Eve is now lost to history. This is because there is no clear evidence for either Hebrew or Aramaic being the language of Adam and Eve. It's possible that they spoke a language that is now extinct. Whatever the case may be, we cannot say for sure what language Adam and Eve spoke. We can only speculate based on the evidence that we have.

What religion was Jesus?

Jesus was a Jewish man who lived in first-century Judea. His birth, ministry, and death occurred during a time of great religious and political turmoil in the land. The Roman Empire ruled Judea and had appointed Herod the Great as the king over the Jews. Herod was not a Jew, but he was a descendant of Esau, the brother of Jacob (from whom the tribes of Israel descended). The Jews were divided between those who supported Herod and those who opposed him. The Gospels tell us that Jesus was born in Bethlehem, a small village in Judea. His parents, Mary and Joseph, were both Jewish. As a young man, Jesus began preaching throughout Judea. He quickly gained a large following of people who were drawn to his message of love, forgiveness, and redemption. During his ministry, Jesus often clashed with the religious leaders of his day. They saw him as a threat to their power and authority. The conflict came to a head when Jesus cleansed the Temple, overturning the tables of the moneychangers and driving out the animals. This act angered the religious leaders and they began to plot Jesus' death. Jesus was arrested and brought before the Roman governor, Pontius Pilate. Pilate found no fault in Jesus and tried to release him, but the Jewish leaders insisted that he be put to death. So, Pilate reluctantly handed Jesus over to be crucified. Jesus' death on the cross was a fulfillment of prophecy. He died as a sacrificial lamb, taking on the sins of the world. His death conquerored death, and through his resurrection, Jesus offers us eternal life.

What does Allah mean in the Bible?

The word "Allah" is used in the Bible to refer to the one true God. It is used in both the Old and New Testaments, and is the same word that is used in the Quran. The word "Allah" is derived from the Arabic word for "God" (الله). This word is used by Arabs of all religions, including Christians and Jews. The word "Allah" was also used by the early Christians in Arabia. The use of the word "Allah" in the Bible is not an accident. It is a deliberate choice by the translators to maintain the accuracy of the text. The word "God" in the Bible can be translated as "Elohim" or "Yahweh", but these words do not have the same meaning as "Allah". "Elohim" is a plural word, and "Yahweh" is the personal name of God. Neither of these words accurately represents the one true God who is both eternal and perfect. The word "Allah" is the best word to use when translating the Bible into Arabic. It is a word that is understood by Arabs of all religions, and it accurately represents the one true God.

What is the ending of the Bible?

The word "Easter" appears in the Bible only once, in the book of Acts. The story of Easter is found in the New Testament of the Bible. Easter is the day that Jesus rose from the dead. The Bible does not give a specific date for the crucifixion or the resurrection. However, we know that Jesus died on the cross on a Friday, and rose from the dead on Sunday. Because of this, we celebrate Easter on the first Sunday after the first full moon after the Spring Equinox. The story of Easter starts with Jesus, who was a man who lived in the Middle East over 2,000 years ago. Jesus was a carpenter, and he also preached about God to the people. Some people believed in what Jesus said, and others did not. The people who did not believe in Jesus thought that he was a troublemaker, and they decided to kill him. Jesus was crucified on a cross. This was a common punishment at the time. After Jesus died, he was buried in a tomb. On the third day, Jesus rose from the dead. His disciples were very surprised to see him alive again. Easter is a very important day for Christians. It is a day to remember that Jesus died for our sins, and that he rose from the dead. This shows us that there is life after death, and that we can have eternal life if we believe in Jesus.

Easter is a time of new beginnings. It is a time to reflect on the past and celebrate the future. It is a time to come together and celebrate the hope that springs eternal.

Where is Jesus crown of thorns now?

Most Christians believe that Jesus was crucified with a crown of thorns on His head. The Bible does not say exactly where this crown of thorns came from, but there are a few theories. One theory is that the crown of thorns was made from the same plant that was used to make the hyssop (a type of plant) that was used to sprinkle blood on the doorposts during the Passover (Exodus 12:22). If this is true, then the crown of thorns may have come from the Garden of Gethsemane, where Jesus went to pray the night before His crucifixion (Matthew 26:36). Another theory is that the crown of thorns was brought to Jesus by the Roman soldiers who mocked Him before His crucifixion (Matthew 27:29). It is possible that the soldiers made the crown of thorns themselves, or that they got it from somewhere else. Whatever the case may be, we know that Jesus wore a crown of thorns on His head during His crucifixion. And we know that after His death, His body was taken down from the cross and buried in a tomb (John 19:38-42). So what happened to the crown of thorns? The Bible does not tell us specifically, but there are a few things that we can infer from what we do know. First of all, we know that Jesus' body was taken down from the cross and buried. This would have required removing the crown of thorns from His head. So, it is possible that the crown of thorns was buried with Jesus. Another possibility is that someone took the crown of thorns as a souvenir. This was not an uncommon practice in those days. People would often take a piece of clothing or some other item from a famous person as a way of remember them (or as a way of making money by selling the item). It is also possible that the crown of thorns was destroyed. This is what happened to the cross that Jesus was crucified on (John 19:31). The Bible says that the soldiers who dismantled the cross "burned the wood and divided the clothes among themselves" (John 19:23). So, it is possible that they did the same thing with the crown of thorns. We may never know exactly what happened to the crown of thorns. But we can be sure that it played an important role in God's plan of salvation. Through His death on the cross, Jesus conquered sin and death and offers us eternal life.

Does the True Cross still exist?

The True Cross is the name for the physical remains which, according to tradition, are of the cross upon which Jesus was crucified. There are numerous supposed relics of the True Cross, many of which are claimed to be genuine and have been venerated for centuries. So, does the True Cross still exist? The answer is not as simple as a yes or no. The True Cross relic is one of great importance to Christians, as it is a physical connection to the crucifixion of Jesus. However, the exact location of the True Cross is unknown, and there are many relics that claim to be the True Cross or a part of it. The history of the True Cross is long and complicated, and the relics that claim to be the True Cross are often controversial. In 326, Constantine the Great claimed to have found the True Cross in Jerusalem, and it has been venerated as a Christian relic ever since. However, many scholars have argued that the True Cross could not have been found by Constantine, as the Edict of Milan, which granted official status to Christianity, was not issued until 313. There are many other claims of the True Cross relic, and it is difficult to determine which, if any, are genuine. In the Middle Ages, there were often multiple relics claiming to be the True Cross, and many of these claims were later proven to be fraudulent. The True Cross is a significant relic for Christians, and its exact location is unknown. There are many relics that claim to be the True Cross or a part of it, but it is difficult to determine which, if any, are genuine.

How did Jesus meet his death?

Death is a difficult topic for many people, especially when it comes to the death of Jesus. It is hard to fathom how someone who was so perfect and sinless could die such a horrible death. The Bible tells us that Jesus was tortured and crucified for our sins. He was beaten, had his beard ripped out, and was nailed to a cross. Even though he was in agony, he still prayed for those who were torturing him. He died a slow and painful death, but he did it for our sake. It is hard to understand why Jesus had to die such a horrific death. But we must remember that he was the perfect sacrifice. He was without sin and he loved us unconditionally. When we put our faith in him, we are forgiven and given eternal life. Jesus died so that we could have that life. When we think about the death of Jesus, we should be reminded of how much he loved us. He was willing to go through such pain and suffering for our sake. We need to remember that and show our love for him by living our lives for him.

How many times did Jesus say to forgive?

How many times did Jesus say to forgive? In the Bible, Jesus said to forgive seventy times seven, or seventy-seven times. This is often misinterpreted as meaning that Christians should only forgive seventy-seven people in their lifetime. However, Jesus was teaching that Christians should always be willing to forgive, no matter how many times they are wronged. Christians should forgive because they have been forgiven by God. When we forgive others, we are showing them the same grace and mercy that God has shown us. Forgiveness is not always easy. Sometimes, the person who has wronged us does not even realize it, or they may not be sorry for what they have done. But even when it is difficult, forgiveness is always the right thing to do. We need to forgive because God has forgiven us. When we forgive, we are setting ourselves free from the pain and hurt of the past. We are also showing others the same grace and mercy that God has shown us.

How many times did Jesus speak of his resurrection?

In the Christian tradition, Easter is the day that Jesus rose from the dead. This event is celebrated as the central act of the Christian faith, as it demonstrates that Jesus is both Lord and Savior. Jesus himself spoke of his resurrection on several occasions, both before and after the event itself. One of the clearest examples of this is found in the Gospel of John, Chapter 2. Jesus is speaking to his disciples after he has turned water into wine at a wedding feast. When his mother tells him that they have run out of wine, Jesus replies, "Woman, what does this have to do with me? My hour has not yet come." But then he performs the miracle anyway. Later, when the disciples are with Jesus in the upper room on the night before he is crucified, he again speaks of his impending resurrection. He tells them that he will go ahead of them to prepare a place for them, and that they know the way to where he is going. On the cross, as he is dying, Jesus once more refers to his resurrection. When the criminal who is being crucified alongside him asks Jesus to remember him when he comes into his kingdom, Jesus replies, "Truly I tell you, today you will be with me in paradise." After his resurrection, Jesus appears to his disciples on several occasions. He speaks to them about his mission, which was to die and rise again so that all might have eternal life. In all, Jesus speaks of his resurrection at least four times in the Gospels. This demonstrates the importance that he placed on this event, and its role in his plan for humanity's salvation.

What did Jesus say in the Last Supper?

The Last Supper is one of the most crucial moments in Christian history. It's the final meal that Jesus Christ shared with his disciples before he was crucified. At this meal, Jesus blessed the bread and shared it with his disciples, saying, "Take, eat; this is my body." He then took the cup of wine, blessed it, and shared it with them, saying, "Drink from it, all of you. This is my blood of the covenant, which is poured out for many for the forgiveness of sins." These words are some of the most important in the Christian faith. They establish the sacrament of Communion, which is a central part of many Christian denominations. But what do they mean? "This is my body" One of the key questions about the Last Supper is what exactly Jesus meant when he said "this is my body." Some Christians interpret this as meaning that the bread literally becomes the body of Christ. This is called the doctrine of transubstantiation and is a central tenet of Catholicism. Other Christians interpret Jesus' words symbolically, believing that the bread represents the body of Christ but doesn't actually become it. "This is my blood of the covenant" Jesus' words about the wine are also open to interpretation. Some Christians believe that the wine literally turns into the blood of Christ. This is called the doctrine of consubstantiation and is held by some Lutherans and Anglicans. Other Christians believe that the wine is just a symbol of the blood of Christ. What did Jesus mean? There's no easy answer to this question. It's one of the things that Christians have been debating for centuries. But ultimately, it's up to each individual Christian to decide what they believe.

What day did Jesus do the Last Supper?

The Last Supper is an event that is commemorated by Christians all over the world. It is the day when Jesus Christ shared a meal with his disciples before he was crucified. The day is also significant because it is the day when Jesus instituted the Eucharist. The Eucharist is a sacrament that is central to the Christian faith. The Last Supper is believed to have taken place on the night of Passover. This was a Jewish holiday that commemorated the deliverance of the Israelites from slavery in Egypt. The Last Supper would have been a Passover meal. During the meal, Jesus took bread and blessed it. He then broke the bread and gave it to his disciples, saying, "Take and eat; this is my body." He also took a cup of wine and blessed it. He then gave it to his disciples and said, "Drink from it, all of you. This is my blood of the covenant, which is poured out for many for the forgiveness of sins." The Last Supper was a significant event in the life of Jesus Christ. It was a time when he shared a meal with his disciples and instituted the Eucharist. The day is also significant because it is the day when Jesus was crucified.

The Easter holiday is a special time of year for many people. It is a time to celebrate the resurrection of Jesus Christ and to enjoy time with family and friends. Easter is also a time for giving thanks for all the blessings in our lives.

What is the Bible verse of the Last Supper?

The Bible verse of the Last Supper is from the Gospel of Matthew, chapter 26, verses 26-29. It reads: "And as they were eating, Jesus took bread, and blessed it, and brake it, and gave it to the disciples, and said, Take, eat; this is my body. And he took the cup, and gave thanks, and gave it to them, saying, Drink ye all of it; For this is my blood of the new testament, which is shed for many for the remission of sins. But I say unto you, I will not drink henceforth of this fruit of the vine, until that day when I drink it new with you in my Father's kingdom." This verse is significant because it is the moment that Jesus institute the Eucharist, or Communion. In the Eucharist, Christians believe that they are receiving the body and blood of Christ. This act is a way of remembering Christ's sacrifice for humanity and is a way of uniting Christians around the world.

What is the moral of the story of the Last Supper?

The Last Supper is one of the most famous paintings in the world. The painting depicts the last meal that Jesus shared with his disciples before his crucifixion. The painting has been interpreted in many ways, but one of the most popular interpretations is that it is a story about the importance of forgiveness. The story of the Last Supper is a story about betrayal. Judas, one of Jesus' disciples, betrayed him to the authorities. This act led to Jesus' crucifixion. However, even though Judas betrayed him, Jesus still forgave him. The moral of the story of the Last Supper is that forgiveness is more important than anything else. No matter how much someone has hurt us, we should always forgive them. Forgiveness is what separates us from animals. It is a sign of our humanity. The story of the Last Supper is an important story because it teaches us about the importance of forgiveness. It is a story that we should all remember.

What is the story behind the Last Supper?

Maundy Thursday, also known as the Last Supper, is the final meal that Jesus Christ ate with his disciples before his arrest and crucifixion. This event is commemorated by Christians on Holy Thursday, the day before Good Friday. The Last Supper is recorded in the Gospel of John 13:1-30. Jesus and his disciples are gathered in an upper room, where Jesus shares a final meal and teaches them about servanthood. He washes their feet as an example of how they should serve others. Jesus then predicts his betrayal by Judas Iscariot, and tells the disciples that one of them will betray him. Judas leaves the room, and Jesus shares the bread and wine with his disciples, telling them that the bread is his body and the wine is his blood. This act is known as the institution of the Eucharist, and is a central practice in Christianity. Jesus then shares a final prayer with his disciples, known as the Lord's Prayer. He predicts his arrest and crucifixion, and tells the disciples that they will all scatter. Peter protests, but Jesus tells him that he will deny him three times. The Last Supper is a powerful moment in the life of Jesus Christ, and is remembered by Christians as a central part of their faith. This momentous event is commemorated each year on Holy Thursday.

How long did the Last Supper last?

The Last Supper is one of the most iconic images of Jesus Christ. The scene is often depicted in art and popular culture. But how long did the Last Supper actually last? There is no definitive answer to this question. The Bible does not give a specific time frame for the Last Supper. Some scholars believe that it lasted for several hours, while others believe that it was a much shorter event. There are a few clues that can help us to understand how long the Last Supper might have lasted. For example, we know that Jesus and his disciples were in the upper room of a house in Jerusalem. This suggests that the meal was not a rushed affair. We also know that the Last Supper was a Passover meal. This was a traditional Jewish meal that was eaten over the course of several hours. It is possible that the Last Supper followed this same pattern. Ultimately, we cannot say for sure how long the Last Supper lasted. But it was probably a lengthy event, giving Jesus and his disciples plenty of time to share their final meal together.

What did they eat at the Last Supper?

What did they eat at the last supper? According to the biblical account, they ate lamb, bread, and wine. But there is no mention of what kind of bread or wine they consumed. The last supper was a Jewish Passover meal, which included roasted lamb. It is believed that the disciples were eating unleavened bread, which was common practice during Passover. The wine could have been either red or white, although it is more likely that it was red. In terms of the actual food that was eaten, there is no record of what was on the menu. But given that it was a Jewish Passover meal, it is likely that there was roasted lamb, bread, and wine.

Did Jesus eat at the Last Supper?

The night before Jesus was crucified, he and his disciples gathered together to share a final meal. This meal, which is now known as the Last Supper, is commemorated by Christians around the world. But did Jesus actually eat at the Last Supper? There is no mention of Jesus eating in any of the four gospel accounts of the Last Supper. In fact, the gospel of John specifically states that, before the meal, Jesus said, "I have not eaten anything in these days. I'm hungry!" (John 4:31-32). So it seems unlikely that Jesus actually ate anything at the Last Supper. There are a few possible explanations for why Jesus may not have eaten at the Last Supper. One possibility is that, given the events of the following day, Jesus simply wasn't hungry. He knew he was going to be crucified the next day and may have lost his appetite as a result. Another possibility is that, as the Son of God, Jesus saw the Last Supper as a symbolic act rather than a literal one. In other words, he saw the bread and wine as representing his body and blood, and he didn't feel the need to actually consume them. Whatever the reason, it seems clear that Jesus did not eat at the Last Supper. And, given the importance of the meal to Christians today, that's definitely something to think about.

What is the purpose of Lord's Supper?

The Lord's Supper, also called Communion or the Eucharist, is a Christian sacrament wherein participants eat bread and drink wine in remembrance of Jesus's Last Supper with his disciples. The practice is widely observed across denominations, though the specific details vary. For instance, Catholics believe that the bread and wine becomes the body and blood of Jesus Christ, while Protestant denominations teach that the supper is only a symbolic representation of Christ. The Lord's Supper is a meaningful way for Christians to remember Jesus and his sacrifice. It is also a way to express unity within the Church. When Christians partake in Communion, they are affirming their belief in the death and resurrection of Jesus Christ. This act of remembrance is a way to ensure thatChristians never forget what he did for them. The Lord's Supper is also a chance for Christians to reflect on their own lives and relationships with God. Partaking in Communion is a way to recommit oneself to following Jesus. It is a time for Christians to reflect on their own sins and shortcomings and to ask for forgiveness. The act of taking Communion can also be a way to let go of any grudges or resentments that one may be holding onto. Ultimately, the purpose of the Lord's Supper is to remember Jesus Christ and all that he did for humanity. It is a chance for Christians to reflect on their own lives and to recommit themselves to following Jesus. The Lord's Supper is also a way for Christians to express their unity with one another.

In conclusion, Easter is a time to celebrate the resurrection of Jesus Christ and the hope that he brings for eternal life. It is a time for family, friends, and loved ones to come together and rejoice.

What makes the Last Supper so special?

The Last Supper is one of the most important events in Christianity. It is the meal that Jesus Christ had with his disciples before he was crucified. The Last Supper is said to be the meal that instituted the Eucharist. The Eucharist is the sharing of bread and wine that is central to the Christian faith. The bread and wine represent the body and blood of Christ. When Christians partake in the Eucharist, they are participating in a sacred ritual that unites them with Christ and with one another. The Eucharist is a reminder of Christ's sacrifice and a symbol of the Christian hope for eternal life. The Last Supper is special because it is a reminder of the ultimate sacrifice that Jesus made for humanity. It is also special because it is an opportunity for Christians to come together and remember the promises that they have made to one another. The Eucharist is a reminder that we are all one in Christ.

Who is the woman in the Last Supper?

The woman in the Last Supper is often thought to be Mary Magdalene. This is because of a number of factors, including the fact that she is shown seated at Jesus' feet in many Renaissance paintings of the scene. However, there is no scriptural basis for this identification and it is more likely that the woman is simply a generic figure symbolising the Church. The Last Supper is one of the most famous and well-loved paintings in the world. It depicts the moment when Jesus Christ gathered his disciples together for their final meal before his crucifixion. The painting is full of symbolism and meaning, and has been the subject of much debate and analysis over the centuries. One of the most hotly contested questions about the painting is the identity of the woman seated at Jesus' feet. In many Renaissance paintings of the Last Supper, this figure is identified as Mary Magdalene. This is because Mary was a key figure in the early days of Christianity, and was present at many of the important events in Jesus' life. She was also the first person to witness the Resurrection, and was therefore seen as a key witness to the events of Christ's life. However, there is no scriptural basis for this identification. The only woman mentioned by name in the Gospel accounts of the Last Supper is Mary, the mother of John Mark. And while it is possible that the woman in the painting is intended to be a generic figure symbolising the Church, there is no definitive evidence to support this theory. So who is the woman in the Last Supper? Unfortunately, we may never know for sure. But regardless of her identity, she remains an important figure in one of the most iconic paintings in history.

What did God do in the Last Supper?

The Last Supper is a key event in Christianity, and is remembered and celebrated by Christians all over the world. It is the meal shared by Jesus and his disciples on the night before his crucifixion, and it is at this meal that Jesus institutes the Eucharist. So what did God do at the Last Supper? First and foremost, the Last Supper was a meal shared in love and fellowship. Jesus and his disciples shared bread and wine together, and Jesus washed his disciples' feet. This was an act of love and service, and it reminded his disciples that they should love and serve one another. At the Last Supper, Jesus also gave his disciples a new commandment: to love one another. He told them that by loving one another, they would be obedient to his commandment, and that this love would be the hallmark of his followers. Jesus also spoke about his forthcoming death and resurrection at the Last Supper. He told his disciples that he would be betrayed and killed, but that he would rise again. This was a difficult message for them to Hear, but it was a crucial part of Jesus' teachings. By speaking about his death and resurrection, Jesus was preparing his disciples for the events of Good Friday and Easter Sunday. And finally, at the Last Supper, Jesus institutes the Eucharist. He takes bread and wine, and blesses them, saying that they are his body and blood. This is a key moment in Christian worship, as Christians believe that when they share in the Eucharist, they are sharing in the body and blood of Christ. So what did God do at the Last Supper? He shared a meal with his disciples, he washed their feet, he commanded them to love one another, he spoke about his death and resurrection, and he instituted the Eucharist. In doing all of these things, God was preparing his disciples for the events of Easter, and for their life as followers of Christ.

What did Jesus predict at the Last Supper with his disciples?

At the Last Supper, Jesus predicted that Peter would deny him three times before the rooster crowed. This prediction came true when Peter denied knowing Jesus to a servant girl, to a maid, and to a man.

How was the Last Supper saved?

The Last Supper is one of the most iconic paintings in Western Art, and its story is equally as iconic. The painting depicts the last meal that Jesus Christ shared with his disciples before his arrest and crucifixion. This event is known as the Last Supper, and it is considered to be one of the most important moments in Christian history. The painting itself is incredibly moving, and its story is one that has been retold countless times. But how was this Last Supper saved? The painting was commissioned by Duke Ludovico Sforza and his wife, Beatrice d'Este. They were both huge fans of Leonardo da Vinci, and they wanted him to paint the Last Supper for them. Leonardo agreed, and he began work on the painting in 1495. The painting took Leonardo three years to complete, and it was finished in 1498. It was then installed in the Duke's palace in Milan. The painting remained in the Duke's palace for over 100 years, until it was looted by French troops in 1796. The painting was taken to Paris, where it was displayed in the Louvre Museum. The painting was returned to Milan in 1815, but it was badly damaged by a fire in the Ducal Palace in 1881. The painting was restored, but it was never returned to its original home. The Last Supper was saved again during World War II. The painting was evacuated from Milan to safety in Agnello, in the Italian Alps. It was returned to Milan in 1945, but it was once again damaged, this time by water and humidity. The Last Supper was restored once again, and it is now on display in the refectory of the Convent of Santa Maria delle Grazie in Milan. It is protected by a bulletproof glass case, and it is one of the most visited tourist attractions in Italy. The Last Supper is an iconic painting, and its story is one that has been retold countless times. It is a story of survival, of hope, and of faith.

Where is the Last Supper located today?

The Last Supper, also known as the Passover meal, is traditionally eaten in the upper room of a house, which is known as the "upper room of Caiaphas." This is the room where Judas Iscariot betrayed Jesus Christ, and where the Last Supper took place. The meal is eaten with unleavened bread and wine, and sometimes lamb.

What kind of fish did Jesus eat?

The Bible doesn't give us a specific answer as to what kind of fish Jesus ate during His earthly ministry, but we can make some assumptions based on what we do know. Jesus was a Jewish man, born and raised in Israel. His diet would have been governed by the kosher laws laid out in the Old Testament. These laws state that only certain types of fish are fit for human consumption. The list of approved fish includes carp, salmon, trout, and whitefish. Of these, carp is the most likely candidate for the fish that Jesus ate. Carp is a very common fish in the Sea of Galilee, where Jesus spent much of His time teaching and performing miracles. This type of fish was also a staple in the diet of first-century Jews. While we can't be certain, it's safe to say that Jesus probably ate carp during His ministry. It would have been readily available and in accordance with His religious beliefs.

Easter is a special day for many people. It is a time to be with family, friends, and loved ones. It is a time to reflect on the past year and to look forward to the future. It is a day to celebrate new beginnings. Easter is a day to remember that Jesus Christ is our Lord and Savior.

Did Jesus eat any animals?

Did Jesus eat any animals? The Bible doesn't give a clear answer on this question, but some people think that Jesus may have eaten fish. In the Book of Matthew, Jesus talks to some fishermen and tells them to "cast their nets on the other side" of the boat. After they do, they catch so many fish that their nets start to break. This could be interpreted as a miracle, but it could also be seen as Jesus simply knowing where the fish were. Another possible piece of evidence that Jesus ate fish comes from the fact that he was baptized in the River Jordan. It's likely that there were fish in the river, and Jesus may have eaten some of them. So, while we can't say for sure whether or not Jesus ate animals, it's possible that he did.

Why did Jesus eat fish after his resurrection?

There are a few possible explanations for why Jesus ate fish after his resurrection. One possibility is that he was demonstrating that he was truly resurrected and not a ghost. In the gospel of Luke, Jesus tells his disciples, "Behold my hands and my feet, that it is I myself. Handle me, and see; for a spirit hath not flesh and bones, as ye see me have" (Luke 24:39). So, eating the fish would have been a way of proving to his disciples that he was alive and not a spirit. Another possibility is that Jesus ate fish to show that he had forgiven the disciples for their doubting and unbelief. After all, it was only after the risen Jesus ate fish in their presence that the disciples were convinced that he was alive (Luke 24:41-43). Eating the fish could have been Jesus' way of showing them that he had forgiven them and that they were now back in his good graces. Finally, it's worth noting that Jesus wasn't the only one who ate fish after his resurrection. In the gospel of John, we're told that Jesus prepared a breakfast of fish for his disciples (John 21:9-13). So, eating fish may have simply been a tradition that arose among the early Christians after the resurrection of Jesus. Whatever the reason, it's clear that fish played a significant role in the early days of Christianity.

What fruit did Jesus eat?

The Easter holiday is a time when Christians celebrate the resurrection of Jesus Christ. One of the key symbols of Easter is the Easter egg, which represents new life. Easter eggs are often decorated with brightly colors and are given to children as gifts. Another key symbol of Easter is the Easter bunny. The Easter bunny is a symbol of hope and new beginnings. The Easter bunny brings gifts to children and delivers them to homes on Easter morning. One of the most popular Easter traditions is the Easter egg hunt. This tradition is enjoyed by children and adults alike. The Easter egg hunt is a fun way to find Easter eggs that are hidden around the house or in the yard. Another tradition that is enjoyed by many on Easter Sunday is the Easter meal. The Easter meal is a time to gather with family and friends and enjoy a delicious meal. The Easter meal often includes a variety of delicious dishes, including Easter ham. Easter is a time to celebrate new life and to enjoy time with family and friends. The Easter egg and the Easter bunny are just two of the many symbols of this special holiday. The Easter egg hunt and the Easter meal are two of the most popular traditions that are enjoyed by many on Easter Sunday.

Was Jesus a vegetarian?

Was Jesus a vegetarian? It's a question that has been debated by scholars and historians for centuries. Some say that there is evidence to suggest that Jesus was a vegetarian, while others say that he was not. There is no clear answer, but there are some interesting theories. One theory is that Jesus was a vegetarian because he was a jew. At the time, many jews were vegetarian because they believed that eating meat was unclean. This theory makes sense, but there is no clear evidence to support it. Another theory is that Jesus was a vegetarian because he was a mystic. Mystics often abstained from eating meat because they believed it was a lower vibration than plant-based food. This theory is interesting, but again, there is no clear evidence to support it. The most likely theory is that Jesus was not a vegetarian. In the Bible, there are several instances where Jesus is seen eating meat, including lamb and fish. It's possible that he ate meat on occasion, but it's more likely that he wasn't a vegetarian. So, was Jesus a vegetarian? The answer is unclear. But what we do know is that he was a man who preached love and compassion, and that is something we can all aspire to.

What is the difference between the Last Supper and the Lord's Supper?

The Last Supper and the Lord's Supper are two important events in the Christian faith. The Last Supper was the last meal that Jesus ate with his disciples before he was crucified. The Lord's Supper is a meal that Christians eat to remember and celebrate the sacrifice that Jesus made for them. There are some key differences between the two meals. The Last Supper was a Passover meal, which was a Jewish tradition. The Lord's Supper is a Christian tradition. The Last Supper was a meal that Jesus shared with his disciples before he died. The Lord's Supper is a meal that Christians share to remember Jesus' sacrifice. The Last Supper was a somber occasion. Jesus knew that he was going to be betrayed and crucified, and he shared a meal with his disciples to prepare them for what was to come. The Lord's Supper is a joyful meal. Christians remember the sacrifice that Jesus made for them, and they celebrate the new life that he has given them. The Last Supper and the Lord's Supper are both important meals in the Christian faith. The Last Supper prepared Jesus' disciples for his death, and the Lord's Supper celebrates Jesus' sacrifice.

How do you explain the Lord's Supper to a child?

The Lord's Supper is a special meal that Christians eat to remember what Jesus did for us. Jesus died on the cross to forgive our sins. When we eat the bread and drink the wine, we remember that Jesus died for us. It can be hard to explain the Lord's Supper to a child. One way to explain it is to say that when we eat the bread and drink the wine, we are remembering what Jesus did for us. We are also participating in a special meal that Jesus shared with his friends before he died. The Lord's Supper is a very special meal for Christians. It is a time for us to remember what Jesus did for us and to thank him for everything.

What does the bread and wine represent?

The bread and wine served during Christian communion is more than just a symbolic gesture. The act of taking communion is a reminder of the sacrificial death of Jesus Christ and His ultimate offering of forgiveness to humanity. Christ's body was broken and His blood was shed so that we could be forgiven and have eternal life. When we partake of the bread and wine, we are reminded that we are participating in something that is much bigger than ourselves. We are remembering the selfless act of love that Jesus displayed by giving His life for us. We are also declaring our own intention to live our lives for Him. The bread and wine is a tangible representation of the spiritual reality of what Christ did for us. It is a way for us to connect with Him on a personal level and to experience His grace and love in a very real way.

Easter is a religious holiday that celebrates the resurrection of Jesus Christ. It is observed by Christians all over the world and is one of the most important days in the Christian calendar. Easter is a time of hope and new beginnings, and is a reminder that no matter what happens in life, there is always the possibility of resurrection and rebirth.

Who is missing from the Last Supper?

The Last Supper is one of the most famous paintings in the world. It is a painting of Jesus and his twelve disciples gathered around a table. But there is one person who is missing from the painting... who is missing from the Last Supper? The Last Supper is a painting of Jesus and his twelve disciples gathered around a table. But there is one person who is missing from the painting... That person is Judas Iscariot, the disciple who betrayed Jesus. According to the Bible, Judas betrayed Jesus for 30 pieces of silver. He then led the soldiers to Jesus so that they could arrest him. So why isn't Judas in the Last Supper painting? The most likely reason is that Judas had already betrayed Jesus by the time the painting was made. This would explain why Judas is not shown in the painting. Another possibility is that the artist simply forgot to include Judas. This seems unlikely, however, as the artist would have been aware of the story of Judas betraying Jesus. Whatever the reason, Judas is missing from the Last Supper painting. And his absence is a reminder of the betrayal that led to Jesus' crucifixion.

Who is the betrayal in the Last Supper?

The Last Supper is one of the most iconic moments in the Bible. It is the story of Jesus and his disciples sharing a meal together before Jesus is betrayed by Judas. This moment has been captured in art, literature, and film throughout history. But who is the real betrayer in this story? Many people believe that Judas is the betrayer because he is the one who betrayed Jesus to the authorities. But Judas was not the only one who betrayed Jesus. All of the disciples betrayed Jesus in some way. Peter denied knowing Jesus when he was questioned by the authorities. This was a betrayal of Jesus because Peter was supposed to be a follower of Jesus. The other disciples also betrayed Jesus by deserting him when he was arrested. They were supposed to be standing by him, but they all ran away. So, if we're looking for the betrayer in the Last Supper, we could say that it was Judas because he betrayed Jesus to the authorities. But we could also say that it was all of the disciples because they all betrayed Jesus in some way.

Who betrayed in Last Supper?

In the Last Supper, Judas Iscariot betrays Jesus Christ by handing him over to the authorities. This event leads to Jesus' arrest, trial, and crucifixion. Judas' betrayal is a key moment in the Biblical story and has been the subject of much debate and analysis over the years. There are many theories about why Judas betrayed Jesus. Some say that Judas was simply following orders from the religious leaders of the time, who were opposed to Jesus' teachings. Others believe that Judas was feeling guilty about his own role in Jesus' ministry and thought that betraying him would somehow make things right. Whatever the reason, Judas' act of betrayal has had a profound impact on Christianity and the world. The Last Supper is one of the most famous paintings in the world, and Judas' betrayal is a key moment in the story. In the painting, Judas is shown with a bag of silver, which was the payment he received for betraying Jesus. This image of Judas has become synonymous with betrayal. The betrayal of Jesus by Judas Iscariot is a key moment in the Bible and has been the subject of much debate and analysis over the years.

What is a fun fact about the Last Supper?

Did you know that the Last Supper was actually a Passover meal? That means that Jesus and his disciples were eating lamb, bitter herbs, and unleavened bread. And, according to Jewish tradition, they were also eating lots of wine! Passover is a holiday that commemorates the Exodus from Egypt. It's a time when Jews remember their ancestors who were slaves in Egypt and celebrate their freedom. The Last Supper was Jesus' last meal before he was crucified, and it's a powerful reminder of his love and sacrifice for all of humanity.

What damaged the Last Supper?

When Judas Iscariot betrayed Jesus Christ to the authorities, he did not just damage the Last Supper, he destroyed it. The Last Supper was a sacred meal shared by Jesus and his closest disciples. It was a time of love, fellowship, and communion. But when Judas betrayed Jesus, he also betrayed the Last Supper. Judas' betrayal damaged the Last Supper in two ways. First, it destroyed the unity and fellowship of the group. Second, it broke the trust between Jesus and his disciples. The group at the Last Supper was united by their shared love for Jesus. But Judas' betrayal broke that unity. His betrayal divided the group and created mistrust among the disciples. The trust between Jesus and his disciples was also broken by Judas' betrayal. Judas was supposed to be one of the closest disciples to Jesus. But he betrayed Jesus for money. This broke the trust between them. The Last Supper was a sacred meal. But Judas' betrayal damage it in two ways. He destroyed the unity of the group and he broke the trust between Jesus and his disciples.

What is the true meaning of the Eucharist?

There are many different interpretations of the Eucharist, and what it represent to each individual. To some, the Eucharist is simply a way to remember Jesus Christ and his sacrifice. Others believe that the Eucharist is actually the body and blood of Christ, and thus is a physical representation of his sacrifice. There are many different belief surrounding the Eucharist, but what is the true meaning of this sacrament? The word "Eucharist" comes from the Greek word "eucharistia", which means "thanksgiving". The Eucharist is a way for Christians to give thanks for the sacrifice that Jesus Christ made for them. It is also a way for Christians to remember the last supper that Jesus had with his disciples, where he shared the bread and wine with them. The Eucharist is a sacrament that is often seen as the most important sacrament in the Catholic Church. This is because the Eucharist is seen as the body and blood of Christ. Catholics believe that when they receive the Eucharist, they are actually receiving the body and blood of Christ. This is a very powerful belief, as it means that Catholics are able to physically receive Christ into their bodies. The Eucharist is a very special and important sacrament to many Christians. It is a way to remember the sacrifice that Jesus made for us, and it is also a way to receive Christ into our own bodies.

What is the difference between Eucharist and Communion?

The Eucharist is the central Christian sacrament in which Christians partake of the body and blood of Christ. The word "Eucharist" comes from the Greek word for "thanksgiving." Communion is a related but broader term that refers to the act of sharing in the body and blood of Christ. It is often used to refer to the Eucharist, but it can also refer to other aspects of Christian unity, such as sharing in the Lord's Supper or participating in the fellowship of the church. The Eucharist is a sacrament, an outward and visible sign of an inward and invisible grace. In the Eucharist, Christians partake of the body and blood of Christ in order to receive forgiveness for their sins and to be united with Christ and one another. The Eucharist is a memorial of Christ's sacrifice on the cross, and it is also a foretaste of the heavenly banquet that will come when Christ returns. Communion is a broader term that can refer to the Eucharist or to other acts of Christian unity. When used in reference to the Eucharist, communion refers to the act of sharing in the body and blood of Christ. Communion can also refer to other aspects of Christian unity, such as sharing in the Lord's Supper or participating in the fellowship of the church.

Events such as Easter bring families together and offer a time of reflection. It is also a time to celebrate new beginnings. For many, Easter is a religious holiday that commemorates the resurrection of Jesus Christ. For others, it is a time to celebrate the coming of spring. However you celebrate, Easter is a special time of year.

What do Catholics mean by Eucharist?

The Catholic Church teaches that the Eucharist is the body, blood, soul, and divinity of Jesus Christ. In other words, when Catholics partake in the Eucharist, they are consuming Jesus Christ himself. This is a hard concept for many non-Catholics to understand because it goes against the grain of what we traditionally think about Communion. The word "Eucharist" comes from the Greek word for "thanksgiving." This is fitting because, as Catholics believe, the Eucharist is the greatest act of thanksgiving that a person can offer to God. When we eat the Eucharist, we are not simply consuming bread and wine, we are consuming the very thing that God gave us out of love: His Son. As Christians, we are called to imitate Christ in every way. And what better way to imitate Christ than to consume his body and blood? When we partake in the Eucharist, we are uniting ourselves with Christ in the most intimate way possible. We are literally consuming his very being. This is a hard concept for many to wrap their heads around, but it is the central mystery of our faith. And it is a mystery that we are called to contemplate and grow in our understanding of throughout our lives.

What happens in the Eucharist?

The Eucharist is the most important sacrament in the Catholic Church. It is the sacrament that unites us with Christ and with each other. The Eucharist is a meal that we share with Christ and with each other. It is a meal that is celebrating the Passover of Jesus Christ. When we partake of the Eucharist, we are receiving the Body and Blood of Christ. This is a sacred and mystical act that has been part of the Church since its very beginning. Christ instituted the Eucharist at the Last Supper. When we partake of the Eucharist, we are uniting ourselves with Christ in a very special way. The Eucharist is a sacred meal, but it is also a communal meal. We are not only uniting ourselves with Christ, but we are also uniting ourselves with each other. The Eucharist is a sign of our unity with each other and with Christ. When we partake of the Eucharist, we are called to remember those who are in need. We are called to think of those who are hungry, those who are sick, those who are in prison. We are called to remember that we are all one body in Christ. The Eucharist is a meal, but it is also a sacrifice. When we offer the Eucharist to God, we are offering our very selves. We are offering our bodies and our blood. We are offering our whole selves to God. The Eucharist is a sign of our love for God. It is a sign of our unity with Christ. It is a sign of our unity with each other. It is a sign of our willingness to offer our very selves to God.

What is the main purpose of the Eucharist?

The Eucharist, also called the Lord's Supper, is the central act of Christian worship. It is a meal where bread and wine are shared, and is seen as a symbol of Jesus' sacrifice. The Eucharist is seen as a way to remember what Jesus did for us, and to show our thanks for his gift of eternal life. The main purpose of the Eucharist is to remember Jesus and what he did for us. It is also seen as a way of thanksgiving for his gift of eternal life. The Eucharist is a sign of our unity with God and with each other, and it is a way of expressing our love for God.

What did Jesus say about the Eucharist?

Most Christians believe that the Eucharist, also known as Communion or the Lord's Supper, is a sacred meal that Jesus commanded his followers to partake in. "Do this in remembrance of me," Jesus is recorded as saying in the Bible, according to the book of Luke (22:19). And, in the book of Corinthians, he says, "The cup of blessing that we bless, is it not a participation in the blood of Christ? The bread that we break, is it not a participation in the body of Christ?" (1 Corinthians 10:16). So what did Jesus mean when he spoke those words? And what does the Eucharist represent for Christians today? There is no one answer to those questions since Christians have a wide range of beliefs about the Eucharist. Some believe that the bread and wine used in the Eucharist are just symbols of Jesus' body and blood. Others believe that the bread and wine actually become the body and blood of Jesus Christ through a process called transubstantiation. Regardless of what people believe about the Eucharist, most Christians agree that it is a significant part of their faith. For many, taking communion is a way to remember and honor Jesus Christ. It is also seen as a way to become closer to God. Some churches have a specific liturgy or order of service for taking communion. But, generally, the bread and wine are shared among the congregation. After everyone has received the Eucharist, they may say a prayer or recite a bible verse together. The Eucharist is a significant part of many people's faith, but there is no one answer to what it means. Just as Jesus said, "Do this in remembrance of me," each person has their own interpretation of what the Eucharist represents.

Why do Protestants not believe in the Eucharist?

There are a number of reasons why Protestants do not believe in the Eucharist. The first is that they do not believe that the bread and wine actually become the body and blood of Christ. They believe that the bread and wine are just symbols of Christ's body and blood. Another reason is that Protestants believe that the Bible does not teach that the bread and wine become the body and blood of Christ. They believe that the Bible teaches that Jesus is the only sacrifice for sin and that there is no need for another sacrifice. Protestants also believe that the Eucharist is not a necessary part of Christian worship. They believe that Christian worship should be focused on God, not on a physical object. finally, many Protestants believe that the Catholic Church has corrupted the meaning of the Eucharist. They believe that the Catholic Church has added man-made traditions and ceremonies to the Eucharist that are not found in the Bible.

Is the Eucharist just the bread?

The Eucharist, also known as Holy Communion or the Lord's Supper, is a central part of Christian worship. But what is it, and what does it mean? Some Christians believe that the Eucharist is simply a symbolic meal, a reminder of Jesus' sacrifice on the cross. Others believe that the bread and wine actually become the body and blood of Christ, a view known as transubstantiation. So which is it? Is the Eucharist just a symbol, or is it something more? There is no simple answer, because there is a great deal of debate on this topic within the Christian community. However, there are a few things we can say for sure. Firstly, it is important to remember that the Eucharist is a sacrament, an outward and visible sign of an inward and spiritual grace. It is a way for us to remember and celebrate Jesus' self-offering love. Secondly, the Eucharist is a communal meal. It is not simply a individual act of eating and drinking, but an opportunity for us to come together as a community and remember our shared life in Christ. Lastly, the Eucharist is a meal of thanksgiving. In giving thanks for all that God has done for us, we remember that we are part of something much larger than ourselves. So what does all this mean? The Eucharist is a complex and rich symbol of our faith. It is a reminder of who we are and whose we are, a sign of our communion with Christ and with one another. It is a meal of thanksgiving, in which we give thanks for all that God has done for us.

Is Jesus only present in the Eucharist?

The Eucharist is the central act of worship in the Catholic Church, and is often seen as the most important aspect of our faith. Jesus is said to be present in the Eucharist, and this is a major reason why Catholics believe that the Eucharist is such a special and important sacrament. However, some people may ask whether Jesus is really present in the Eucharist, or whether he is only present in our hearts and minds. After all, Jesus is not physically present in the Eucharist, and we cannot see him. So how can we be sure that he is really there? The answer lies in understanding what the Eucharist is and what it means to us as Catholics. The Eucharist is not just a physical thing, it is also a spiritual reality. When we receive the Eucharist, we are not just taking in bread and wine, we are also taking in the body and blood of Christ. This means that we are taking in the very life of Jesus – his love, his strength, his hope. And when we do this, we are transformed. We become more like Jesus, and we are filled with his presence. So, while we cannot see Jesus in the Eucharist, we can feel his presence within us. And this is what makes the Eucharist so special and so important to us as Catholics. It is a tangible way of feeling the presence of Jesus in our lives, and of receiving his love and strength.

The author argues that easter is a great holiday for Christians and non-Christians alike. She cites several reasons for this, including the fact that it is a time for family, friends, and community. She also notes that easter is a time for religious reflection and for celebrating the hope of new beginnings.

How is the Eucharist different between Catholic and Protestant?

The word "Eucharist" comes from the Greek word for "thanksgiving." It is also known as the Lord's Supper or Holy Communion. Catholics believe that the Eucharist is the body, blood, soul, and divinity of Jesus Christ. This belief is based on the doctrine of transubstantiation. Transubstantiation is the belief that the bread and wine used in the Eucharist change into the body and blood of Jesus Christ. Protestants do not believe in transubstantiation. Instead, they believe that the bread and wine are symbols of the body and blood of Jesus Christ.

Do Catholics believe Jesus is in the Eucharist?

The Easter holiday is a time when Christians celebrate the resurrection of Jesus Christ. For Catholics, this event is commemorated by the Eucharist, which is a special meal that is shared by the community. The bread and wine that are used during the Eucharist represent the body and blood of Christ, and Catholics believe that when they consume these, they are receiving the real presence of Jesus. This belief is based on the teachings of Christ himself, who said that the bread and wine were his body and blood (Luke 22:19-20). The Eucharist is a central part of Catholic worship, and it is seen as a way to connect with the risen Christ. When Catholics take part in the Eucharist, they are reminded of Jesus' sacrifice and are united with him in a special way. This sacrament is seen as a source of strength and comfort, and it is an important part of the Easter celebrations.

Is Eucharist and Holy Mass the same?

Eucharist and Holy Mass are two terms that are often used interchangeably, but they actually refer to two different things. The Eucharist is the central act of Christian worship, in which Christians share bread and wine as a sign of their shared life with God. The word "Eucharist" comes from the Greek word for "thanksgiving." Holy Mass is the name given to the Eucharistic liturgy in the Catholic tradition. In other words, it is the name for the specific form of worship that Catholics use to celebrate the Eucharist. The word "Mass" comes from the Latin word for "dismissal" (as in, the dismissal of the congregation at the end of the service). So, while the Eucharist is the central act of Christian worship, Holy Mass is the specific form of worship that Catholics use to celebrate the Eucharist.

How long does the Eucharist last?

The Eucharist, also known as Holy Communion, is a sacrament in which Christians eat bread and drink wine in remembrance of Jesus Christ. The bread and wine represent the body and blood of Christ, and the Eucharist is considered to be a sacred meal. There are different opinions on how long the Eucharist should last, but most Christians believe that it should be a part of a longer worship service. The Eucharist is a sacred meal for Christians because it is a reminder of Jesus Christ and his sacrifice for our sins. When we eat the bread and drink the wine, we are reminded of Jesus' body and blood that were shed for us. The Eucharist is also a way for us to show our thanks and praise to God. There are different opinions on how long the Eucharist should last, but most Christians believe that it should be a part of a longer worship service. The Eucharist is a sacred meal, and it is a time for us to remember what Jesus did for us. We should take our time in eating the bread and drinking the wine, and we should also spend time talking to God and thanking him for his Son.

Can you touch the Eucharist?

The Eucharist, also known as Holy Communion or the Lord's Supper, is a Christian sacrament commemorating the Last Supper of Jesus Christ and his disciples. The bread and wine used in the Eucharist are consecrated by a priest and are believed by many Christians to be transformed into the body and blood of Christ. However, the Catholic Church teaches that the bread and wine remain unchanged after consecration. They only become the body and blood of Christ in a spiritual sense. This is known as transubstantiation. So, can you touch the Eucharist? The short answer is no. The Catholic Church believes that the Eucharist is the body, blood, soul, and divinity of Jesus Christ. Therefore, it is to be treated with the utmost respect. The Catechism of the Catholic Church states that the Eucharist is "a sacrament of love, a sign of unity, a bond of charity, a Paschal banquet 'in which Christ is consumed, the mind is filled with grace, and a pledge of future glory is given to us.'" Because of this, the Church urges everyone to receive the Eucharist with reverence and devotion. This means that we should not approach the Eucharist casually or without respect. When receiving the Eucharist, we should genuflect (kneel down) before receiving it. We should also use our right hand to receive the host, and raise it to our mouth. It is also considered proper etiquette to say "Amen" after receiving the Eucharist. So, while you can't touch the Eucharist, you can receive it reverently and with devotion. By doing so, you are participating in a sacred moment that unites you with Jesus Christ and the Church.

Does the Eucharist forgive sins?

The Eucharist is one of the most central and important aspects of the Catholic faith. Christ himself said that the Eucharist is "his body, given for you" and "his blood, shed for you". From this we learn that the Eucharist is not only a sign of Christ's love for us, but also a source of his grace. When we receive the Eucharist, we are forgiven of our sins. This is because the Eucharist is not just a symbol of Christ's love, but also a source of his grace. Christ himself said that the Eucharist is "his body, given for you" and "his blood, shed for you". When we receive Christ's body and blood in the Eucharist, we are receiving forgiveness for our sins. The Eucharist is not just a symbols of Christ's love, but also a source of his grace. Christ himself said that the Eucharist is "his body, given for you" and "his blood, shed for you". By receiving the Eucharist, we are receiving forgiveness for our sins.

Why is the Eucharist so powerful?

The Eucharist is a powerful sacrament because it is the re-enactment of Jesus' sacrificial death on the cross. When we partake in the Eucharist, we are reminded of Jesus' ultimate act of love for us. The Eucharist unites us with Christ and with one another. It is a physical expression of our oneness with God. The Eucharist is a powerful reminder of the cost of our redemption. Jesus didn't simply die; he was tortured and humiliated first. He did this because he loves us and he wants us to be with him in eternity. The Eucharist is a way for us to connect with Jesus on a personal level and to remember what he did for us. The Eucharist is also a powerful way to resist temptation. When we are physically and spiritually nourished by the Eucharist, we are less likely to give in to temptation. The Eucharist strengthens us to live a life that is pleasing to God. In addition, the Eucharist is a reminder of the Resurrection. Jesus' death was not the end of the story; he rose from the dead, defeating death once and for all. When we partake in the Eucharist, we proclaim our belief in the Resurrection and our hope for eternal life. The Eucharist is a powerful sacrament because it is a physical expression of our oneness with God. When we partake in the Eucharist, we are reminded of Jesus' ultimate act of love for us. The Eucharist unites us with Christ and with one another. It is a way for us to connect with Jesus on a personal level and to remember what he did for us. The Eucharist is also a reminder of the Resurrection. Jesus' death was not the end of the story; he rose from the dead, defeating death once and for all. When we partake in the Eucharist, we proclaim our belief in the Resurrection and our hope for eternal life.

Easter is a religious holiday that celebrates the resurrection of Jesus Christ. It is also a time for family and friends to get together and celebrate. Easter is a time of hope and new beginnings.

What are three things about the Eucharist?

The Eucharist is a sacrament of the Catholic Church in which Christ's body and blood are consumed by the faithful. It is considered to be the source and summit of the Christian life. Here are three things to know about the Eucharist: 1. The Eucharist is a sacred meal. The Eucharist is not just a meal, but a sacred meal. It is a way for us to come together as a community and remember what Christ has done for us. When we eat the bread and drink the wine, we are reminded of Christ's sacrifice for us on the cross. The Eucharist is a way for us to connect with Christ and with one another. 2. The Eucharist is a gift from Christ. The Eucharist is not something we earn or deserve. It is a gift from Christ. Christ invites us to come to him and receive his body and blood. When we participate in the Eucharist, we are accepting Christ's gift of himself. 3. The Eucharist is a source of strength. The Eucharist is a source of strength for us as Christians. It is a way for us to remember Christ's love for us and to be reminded of his sacrifice. When we participate in the Eucharist, we are filled with Christ's grace and strength.

Why did Jesus create the Eucharist?

The Eucharist is a deeply significant event in Christian theology and practice, but why did Jesus create it? The act of taking bread and wine and sharing them with others is a symbolic and powerful way to express unity and community, but there must be more to it than that. Christian tradition teaches that the Eucharist is the re-enactment of the Last Supper, which Jesus shared with his disciples before his crucifixion. At that meal, Jesus took bread and wine, blessed them, and said that they were his body and blood. He then asked his disciples to eat and drink in remembrance of him. So, the Eucharist is first and foremost a way for Christians to remember and re-experience the last moments that Jesus spent with his friends before his death. But it is also much more than that. As Christians remember and partake in the Eucharist, they are also participating in the act of redemption. In the act of taking bread and wine and sharing them, Christians are reminded of Jesus' sacrifice for them on the cross. And as they eat and drink, they are proclaiming that they believe in Jesus' resurrection. The Eucharist is thus a way for Christians to proclaim their faith, to remember Jesus' sacrifice, and to celebrate his resurrection. But it is also a way for them to experience unity with one another and with God. When Christians eat and drink together in the Eucharist, they are reminded that they are all part of the same body, the body of Christ. The Eucharist is a powerful and sacred act that has been at the heart of Christian worship for centuries. It is a way for Christians to remember and experience the last moments of Jesus' life, to proclaim their faith, and to celebrate their unity with one another and with God.

Do Christians eat the Eucharist?

The Easter holiday is a time when Christians commemorate the resurrection of Jesus Christ. One of the ways they do this is through the consumption of the Eucharist, which is also known as communion. The Eucharist is a sacrament in which Christians believe that the body and blood of Jesus Christ are present. In the New Testament, Jesus institutes the Eucharist at the Last Supper, telling his disciples to eat his body and drink his blood. Because the Eucharist is such an important sacrament, there is a lot of debate surrounding it. Some people believe that Christians actually consume the body and blood of Jesus Christ during the Eucharist. Others believe that the Eucharist is merely a symbolic act. There is no clear answer as to whether or not Christians actually consume the body and blood of Jesus Christ during the Eucharist. However, what is clear is that the Eucharist is a very important sacrament to Christians. It is a way for them to remember the sacrifice that Jesus made for them and to celebrate his resurrection.

What Bible verse is the Eucharist?

The Eucharist is a biblical term referring to the last supper that Jesus Christ had with his disciples before he was crucified. This event is recorded in the gospels of Matthew, Mark, and Luke. The Eucharist is also mentioned in Paul's first letter to the Corinthians. In this letter, Paul tells the Corinthians that the Eucharist is a sacred mystery and that it is a memorial of Christ's sacrifice. The word "Eucharist" comes from the Greek word for "thanksgiving." This word is used because the Eucharist is a thanksgiving meal. Jesus gave thanks for the bread and wine before he shared it with his disciples. This act of giving thanks is called the Eucharistic Prayer. The Eucharist is a very important part of the Christian faith. It is a reminder of what Jesus did for us and a way for us to remember his sacrifice. The Eucharist is also a way for us to show our thankfulness to God.

What are the 4 ways Jesus is present in the Eucharist?

When Catholics partake in the Eucharist, they believe that they are receiving the literal body and blood of Jesus Christ. This is a mystery that has been difficult for many to understand and accept. However, there are four ways that Catholics believe Jesus is present in the Eucharist. The first way is called the Real Presence. This means that Jesus is truly present in the Eucharist and is not just a symbol. His body and blood are actually present and are not just substitutes. The second way is called Transubstantiation. This is the belief that the bread and wine actually change into the body and blood of Christ. This happens through the power of the Holy Spirit and is a miraculous event. The third way is called Sacramental Presence. This means that Jesus is present in the Eucharist through his body and blood, but also through his Spirit. This is possible because Jesus is a divine being and his Spirit is everywhere. The fourth and final way is called Mystical Presence. This is the belief that Jesus is present in the Eucharist in a way that goes beyond our understanding. We believe that he is present in a way that is beyond time and space. This is the most difficult way to understand but it is also the most fascinating. Whether you believe in one, two, three, or all four of these ways, there is no doubt that the Eucharist is a special and sacred event. Catholics believe that they are receiving the body and blood of Jesus Christ and this is a powerful and moving experience.

Which Christians do not celebrate the Eucharist?

There are a number of Christians who do not celebrate the Eucharist, or Holy Communion. These include some who believe that the bread and wine of communion are merely symbols, and that the act is not a true sacrament. Others believe that the Eucharist is a sacrament, but that Christ is not physically present in the bread and wine. Those who do not believe that the bread and wine are the body and blood of Christ may still participate in communion services as a means of rememberance or as a way of affirming their belief in the oneness of the body of Christ. For some, communion is a way of partake in a corporate act of worship, even if they do not believe in the real presence of Christ. There are a number of reasons why Christians may choose not to participate in communion. Some may feel that they are not yet ready to receive communion, or that they need to confess their sins first. Others may feel that they are not yet able to fully understand the mystery of the Eucharist. For some, the act of communion may be seen as an empty ritual if they do not believe in the real presence of Christ. Whatever the reason, there are a number of Christians who do not partake in communion. This does not mean that they are any less Christian than those who do, but simply that they have a different understanding of the Eucharist.

Why did Luther reject the Eucharist?

Easter is one of the most important holidays in the Christian faith, commemorating the resurrection of Jesus Christ. For many Christians, the Easter holiday is a time of joy and celebration. However, for some, like Martin Luther, Easter is a time of reflection and contemplation. Luther rejected the Eucharist, or communion, because he believed that it was a false sacrament. Luther was a strong believer in the Bible and the authority of Scripture. He believed that all Christians should be able to read and interpret the Bible for themselves. This is one of the reasons why Luther rejected the Eucharist. He did not believe that the Bible taught that the bread and wine used in communion were the actual body and blood of Christ. Rather, he believed that they were only symbols. Luther also believed that the Eucharist was a false sacrament because of the way it was being administered in his day. He saw that many people were coming to communion without first confessing their sins. They were simply taking the bread and wine and not receiving forgiveness. In Luther's eyes, this was not true communion. Luther's rejection of the Eucharist was one of the key issues that led to the split between the Catholic and Protestant churches. It is still a controversial issue today. Many Protestants, particularly Lutherans, continue to practice communion, while other Protestants have rejected it altogether.

The Easter holiday is a special time for many people. It is a time to celebrate the resurrection of Jesus Christ and to give thanks for God's blessings. Easter is also a time for family and friends to gather together and enjoy each other's company. For many, the Easter holiday is a time of joy and happiness.

What is the significance of Eucharist in the Catholic church?

The Eucharist is the most important sacrament in the Catholic Church. It is the sacrament that Jesus instituted at the Last Supper, and it is the sacrament that gives us the Body and Blood of Christ. The Eucharist is a sacrificial meal, and it is the only sacrament that is required for salvation. The Eucharist is a sacrament of Christ's love. It is a sacrament that brings us into union with Christ. We believe that when we receive the Eucharist, we are receiving the very body and blood of Christ. This is a profound mystery, and it is one of the things that makes the Eucharist so special. Christ is really and truly present in the Eucharist, and we believe that we are receiving his very body and blood. The Eucharist is a sacrificial meal. When we receive the Eucharist, we are participating in the one sacrifice of Christ. We believe that Christ sacrificed his body and blood on the cross for our salvation, and that by receiving the Eucharist, we are participating in that sacrifice. The Eucharist is the sacrament that gives us the Body and Blood of Christ. This is a great mystery, but it is one of the things that makes the Eucharist so special. Christ is really and truly present in the Eucharist, and we believe that we are receiving his very body and blood. The Eucharist is the most important sacrament in the Catholic Church because it is the sacrament that Jesus instituted at the Last Supper. It is the sacrament that brings us into union with Christ, and it is the sacrament that gives us the Body and Blood of Christ. The Eucharist is a sacrificial meal, and it is the only sacrament that is required for salvation.

What is the Eucharist and what is its significance to Christians?

The Eucharist is the central Christian sacrament in which bread and wine are consecrated and consumed in remembrance of Jesus Christ. The word Eucharist is derived from Greek and means "thanksgiving." Christians believe that the Eucharist is a sacred mystery through which the body and blood of Christ are mystically present to the believer. The Eucharist is commemorated in the Lord's Supper, which is also sometimes called Holy Communion or the Mass. It is a sacrament of the New Covenant, which was instituted by Jesus at the Last Supper before his crucifixion. In the Eucharist, Christians celebrate the sacrificial death and resurrection of Christ, and proclaim his real presence in the bread and wine. The bread and wine of the Eucharist are not just symbols; they are actually the body and blood of Christ, according to the doctrine of transubstantiation. This means that, although the bread and wine retain their outward appearance, their inner substance is transformed into the body and blood of Christ. This change is brought about by the power of the Holy Spirit and the words of the priest during the Eucharistic Prayer. The Eucharist is a sign of unity among Christians. It is a way of expressing our oneness in Christ. When we partake in the Eucharist, we are proclaiming our faith in the Real Presence of Christ in the bread and wine. We are also confessing our belief in the unity of the Church. The Eucharist is also a meal, and as such, it is a foretaste of the heavenly banquet that awaits us in the Kingdom of God. In the Eucharist, we receive the body and blood of Christ, which are the food and drink of eternal life. receiving these gifts now enables us to share in the life of Christ and to be strengthened in our daily lives. The Eucharist is a source of strength and consolation for Christians. It is a reminder of God's love for us and of our membership in the body of Christ. The Eucharist is also a sign of hope. As we partake of the bread and wine, we are reminded that one day we will share in the heavenly banquet and be united with Christ for all eternity.

What are 2 reasons why the Eucharist is important?

The Eucharist is one of the most important parts of the Christian faith for a number of reasons. First and foremost, it is a reminder of Jesus' sacrifice for humanity. As Jesus Himself said, "This is my body given for you; do this in remembrance of me." (Luke 22:19) In the Eucharist, Christians remember and give thanks for what Jesus did for them. It is also a reminder of the promise of Jesus' return. As Jesus said, "I will not drink from this fruit of the vine from now on until that day when I drink it new with you in my Father's kingdom." (Matthew 26:29) The Eucharist looks forward to the time when all believers will be united with Christ in heaven. In addition to being a remembrance and a promise, the Eucharist is also a source of strength and grace. As Jesus said, "Whoever eats my flesh and drinks my blood has eternal life, and I will raise them up at the last day." (John 6:54) The Eucharist is not just a symbol; it is truly the body and blood of Christ, and as such, it has the power to give us eternal life. It is also a means of grace, giving us the strength to live our lives according to God's will. The Eucharist is thus an incredibly important part of the Christian faith. It is a reminder of Jesus' sacrifice, a promise of His return, and a source of strength and grace. It is a reminder that we are never alone, and that God is always with us.

What is the Eucharist in simple terms?

The Eucharist is a central Christian ritual where bread and wine are consumed. The bread and wine represent the body and blood of Jesus Christ. Christ's body and blood are believed to be present in the bread and wine, making them holy. When Christians partake in the Eucharist, they are essentially consuming the body and blood of Jesus Christ and taking part in his grace. The Eucharist has always been a controversial topic, with different interpretations and practices within Christianity. Some Christians believe that the Eucharist is a purely symbolic act, while others believe that the body and blood of Christ are actually present in the bread and wine. The Catholic Church teaches that the bread and wine are transubstantiated into the body and blood of Christ. This means that the bread and wine retain their physical properties, but their substance is changed into the body and blood of Christ. Critics of the Catholic Church's teaching on transubstantiation argue that it is idolatrous and goes against the teachings of the Bible. Critics also argue that the Catholic Church has changed the meaning of the Eucharist over time. The Catholic Church has responded to these criticisms by stating that the Eucharist is a sacred mystery that cannot be fully understood by human reason. The Eucharist is a central and important part of the Catholic Mass. The Mass is a ritual that commemorates the Last Supper, when Jesus Christ ate with his disciples before his crucifixion. During the Mass, the priest consecrates the bread and wine, which are then consumed by the congregation. The Eucharist is seen as a way to unite Christians with Christ and with each other. The Eucharist is a sacred ritual for Christians and has been a source of controversy and debate throughout the history of Christianity. While the meaning of the Eucharist is still debated, it remains a central and important part of Christian worship.

What does the bread and wine symbolize?

The bread and wine has been a symbol of Christ's body and blood since the Last Supper. The bread symbolizes the body of Christ that was broken for us, and the wine symbolizes the blood that was shed for our sins. This is why we partake of the bread and wine in communion, to remember what Christ did for us. But what does this all mean? Why did Christ have to die for us? And what does the bread and wine really represent? In order to understand the true meaning of the bread and wine, we must first understand the concept of sacrificial love. Christ died for us because he loved us. He loved us so much that he was willing to give up his own life in order to save us from our sins. This is the ultimate act of love. And what do the bread and wine represent? They represent the sacrificial love of Christ. When we partake of the bread and wine, we are reminded of the ultimate sacrifice that Christ made for us. We are reminded of the great love that he has for us. The bread and wine is a symbol of Christ's sacrificial love for us. It is a reminder of the great sacrifice that he made for us. And it is a reminder of the great love that he has for us.

What is the sacrament of the Holy Eucharist summary?

The sacrament of the Holy Eucharist is one of the most important sacraments in the Catholic Church. It is the sacrament that gives us the body and blood of Jesus Christ, and it is the sacrament that unites us with Christ in a special way. The word "Eucharist" comes from the Greek word for "thanksgiving." The Holy Eucharist is a thanksgiving to God for all His blessings. It is also a sacrificial meal in which we offer our sacrifices to God. In the Old Testament, God gave His people the sacrificial system as a way to worship Him. They would offer sacrifices of animals and crops to God, and this was a way for them to thank God for His blessings and to ask for His forgiveness. The ultimate sacrifice is the offering of Jesus Christ on the cross. His body and blood were offered up for the forgiveness of our sins. When we receive the Holy Eucharist, we are receiving the body and blood of Jesus Christ, and we are being united with Him in a special way. The Holy Eucharist is a sacrament that should be taken seriously. It is not a casual meal, and we should not take it lightly. When we receive the Eucharist, we are receiving the body and blood of Jesus Christ, and we are entering into a special relationship with Him.

What is the most important part of the Holy Eucharist?

The Eucharist, also known as Holy Communion or the Lord's Supper, is the central act of worship in the Catholic Church. It is the summit and source of the Christian life, the source and summit of the Church's mission, and the most efficacious sign of Christ's presence. The Eucharist is a fundamental part of Catholic belief because it is seen as the re-presentation of Jesus Christ's sacrifice on the cross. In the act of communion, Catholics believe that they are receiving the body, blood, soul and divinity of Jesus Christ. This act is a memorial of Christ's death and resurrection, and a foretaste of the heavenly banquet to come. The Eucharist is also a sacrificial meal, in which we offer our own lives to God in union with the sacrifice of Jesus Christ. This meal is a foretaste of the heavenly banquet, in which we will share in the banquet of the Lamb in the kingdom of God. The Eucharist is celebrated in the Mass, which is the central act of Catholic worship. The Mass is a rite that is rich in meaning and symbolism, and it is through the Mass that we enter into the mystery of Christ's sacrifice. The Eucharist is the most important part of the Holy Mass because it is the moment when we receive the body and blood of Christ. It is also the moment when we offer our own lives to God in union with the sacrifice of Christ.

Easter is a special time of year for many people. It is a time to celebrate the resurrection of Jesus Christ and to spend time with family and friends. For many, Easter is also a time to reflect on their own personal faith and to make new commitments to living a Christ-centered life. Whether you celebrate Easter in a church service, at an Easter egg hunt, or in your own special way, we hope you have a blessed Easter!

What are 5 significant names that the Eucharist is known by?

The Eucharist has been known by many names throughout history. Here are five of the most significant: 1. The Eucharist is sometimes known as the Lord's Supper. This name reminds us that Jesus instituted the Eucharist at the Last Supper before his crucifixion. The Eucharist is a way for us to remember and celebrate Jesus' sacrifice for us. 2. The Eucharist is also known as the Bread of Life. This name comes from Jesus' words in John 6:35, where he says, "I am the bread of life. Whoever comes to me will never go hungry, and whoever believes in me will never be thirsty." The Eucharist is a way for us to receive Jesus' life-giving body and blood. 3. Another name for the Eucharist is the Holy Communion. This name reminds us that the Eucharist is a way for us to commune with God. We receive Jesus' body and blood, and in doing so, we are united with him and with one another. 4. The Eucharist is sometimes called the Memorial of the Passion. This name reminds us that the Eucharist is a way for us to remember and celebrate Jesus' sacrifice for us. 5. Finally, the Eucharist is also known as the Sacrament of the Body and Blood of Christ. This name reminds us that the Eucharist is a sacred meal in which we receive the very body and blood of Christ.

How the Eucharist does transform a person?

When someone partakes in the Eucharist, they are consuming the body and blood of Christ. This act is often seen as a symbolic gesture, but it can also be seen as something that actually transforms the person consuming it. The Eucharist has been a central part of Christian tradition since the early days of the religion. In the early Church, communion was seen as a way of uniting the body of Christ with the individual believer. The Eucharist was seen as a way of physically consuming the body of Christ and thus becoming one with him. This act was seen as a way of receiving forgiveness and becoming closer to God. As the centuries went on, the Eucharist became increasingly seen as a way of receiving grace from God. The act of consuming the body and blood of Christ was seen as a way of receiving the Holy Spirit. This transformation was seen as a way of becoming more like Christ and living a more godly life. The Eucharist is still a central part of many Christian traditions today. It is seen as a way of uniting with Christ and receiving his grace. For many Christians, the act of consuming the body and blood of Christ is a way of physically and spiritually consuming the grace of God.

What is the power of the Eucharist?

The Eucharist is a sacrament of the Christian faith, in which bread and wine are consecrated and consumed by the faithful. This act is seen as a powerful way to connect with God and to receive His grace. The Eucharist has been a central part of Christian worship since the early days of the Church. In the New Testament, we see Jesus Himself instituting the Eucharist at the Last Supper. And throughout the centuries, Christians have continued to gather around the table to partake in this sacred meal. There are many who see the Eucharist as just a symbol. But for Catholics, the Eucharist is much more than that. We believe that the bread and wine are actually transformed into the body and blood of Christ. This is known as the doctrine of transubstantiation. The Eucharist is a sacrament that brings us into a closer union with Christ. By consuming His body and blood, we are united with Him in a special way. We become more like Him and are better able to follow His example. The Eucharist is also a powerful source of grace. When we receive Communion, we are receiving Christ Himself. And as we receive Him, we are also receiving His grace. This grace gives us the strength to overcome sin and to grow in holiness. The Eucharist is a precious gift that we are privileged to receive. It is a sacrament that brings us closer to Christ and fills us with His grace. May we never take this gift for granted, but may we always approach the Eucharist with reverence and awe.

What are the symbols of the Eucharist?

The Eucharist is a central element of Christian liturgy, and there are a number of symbols associated with it. The bread and wine represent the body and blood of Jesus Christ, and the act of taking them is symbolic of the participant's participation in the body and blood of Christ. The Eucharist is also sometimes known as the "bread of life" or the "cup of salvation", and these names are significant in themselves. The Eucharist is a powerful symbol of the unity of the Church. When we take the bread and wine, we are symbolically uniting ourselves with Christ and with each other. The bread and wine become the body and blood of Christ, and we become one with him. The Eucharist is also a reminder of the key moments in the life of Christ. The Last Supper was the final meal that Jesus shared with his disciples before he was crucified, and the Eucharist is a reminder of that act of sacrifice. When we take the bread and wine, we remember that Christ died for us and that we are forgiven. The Eucharist is also a symbol of hope. In the midst of difficulties and trials, we can remember that Christ is with us, and that he will never leave us. The Eucharist is a reminder that we are never alone, and that we can always find hope in Christ.

What are the lessons of the Eucharist?

The Eucharist is a central mystery of our faith. In it, Christ becomes truly present to us, offering himself as food for our journey to eternal life. In the act of eating his body and drinking his blood, we enter into communion with Christ and become one with him. We also become part of the body of Christ, the Church. The Eucharist is a constant reminder of the love of Christ for us and of our need to love one another. Christ sacrificed himself for us, and in the Eucharist he makes that sacrifice present to us. As we eat his body and drink his blood, we are called to remember that we are called to love one another as he has loved us. The Eucharist is also a reminder of our call to holiness. In receiving the Eucharist, we are called to be purified and to grow in holiness. We are called to live our lives in such a way that we become more like Christ. In the Eucharist, we are given the grace to grow in love and to become holy. These are the lessons of the Eucharist.

What are the benefits of the Eucharist?

The Eucharist is a sacred rite of the Catholic Church that involves the Consecration of the bread and wine, and the subsequent consumption of those items by the communicants. The Eucharist is considered to be a fundamental mystery of the Church, and participation in the Eucharist is seen as a necessary part of the Christian life. There are many benefits of the Eucharist. One of the most important is that it is a way for Christians to remember and celebrate the life, death, and resurrection of Jesus Christ. The Eucharist is a way of making present the sacrifice of Jesus on the cross, and it is through this sacrifice that we are able to receive forgiveness for our sins. Another benefit of the Eucharist is that it is a source of strength and grace for Christians. When we receive the Eucharist, we receive the body and blood of Christ, which gives us the strength to live our lives according to his teachings. In addition, the Eucharist is a source of grace because it is through the Eucharist that we are able to receive the sacraments. The Eucharist is also a sign of unity for Christians. When we participate in the Eucharist, we are affirming our belief that we are all part of the one body of Christ. This unity is something that is essential to the Christian faith, and it is something that is renewed each time we partake in the Eucharist. Ultimately, the benefits of the Eucharist are numerous. It is a way for Christians to remember and celebrate the life of Jesus Christ, it is a source of strength and grace, and it is a sign of unity. The Eucharist is a fundamental mystery of the Church, and participation in the Eucharist is essential to the Christian life.

What is the most important part of the Eucharist and why?

The Eucharist, also known as Holy Communion or the Lord's Supper, is a Christian sacrament in which bread and wine are consumed to remember Jesus Christ's sacrificial death on the cross. The bread and wine represent Christ's body and blood, respectively, and the act of partaking in the Eucharist is seen as a way of uniting with Christ and fellow Christians. So what is the most important part of this sacrament? That depends on who you ask. Some Christians might say that the bread and wine are the most important part, as they are the physical elements that represent Christ's body and blood. Others might say that the act of partaking in the Eucharist is the most important part, as it is a way of symbolic communion with Christ and other believers. Still, others might say that the Eucharist is not about the bread and wine or the act of communion, but about remembering Christ's sacrifice. In this view, the most important part of the Eucharist is the intention with which it is carried out. To remember Christ's sacrifice is to remember His love for us, and to be thankful for the great gift of salvation that He offers. No matter what your view, the Eucharist is a significant and special sacrament in Christianity. It is a time to remember what Christ did for us and to unite with Him and other believers.

Easter is a religious holiday that celebrates the resurrection of Jesus Christ. It is observed by Christians all over the world and is one of the most important holidays in the Christian calendar. On this day, Christians remember and give thanks for the life and teachings of Jesus Christ. Easter is a time of hope and renewal, and a reminder that, despite the challenges we face in life, God's love is always with us.

What is the history of the Eucharist?

The Eucharist is a Christian rite that is considered to be a sacrament by most denominations. It is a reenactment of the Last Supper, which was a meal that Jesus shared with his disciples before his crucifixion. The word "Eucharist" comes from the Greek word for "thanksgiving." The Eucharist has been a part of Christian worship since the early Church. The first recorded instance of the Eucharist being celebrated is from the Didache, a document from the late first or early second century. In the Didache, the Eucharist is referred to as the "breaking of bread." This is most likely a reference to the bread that was broken during the Last Supper. The Eucharist was originally celebrated in private homes, but as the Church grew, it began to be celebrated in public places such as churches. The exact form of the Eucharist has varied throughout history. In the early Church, the Eucharist was usually celebrated with leavened bread and wine. This was in keeping with the Jewish tradition of the Passover meal, which was also a meal that Jesus shared with his disciples. In the Middle Ages, the Eucharist began to be celebrated with unleavened bread and wine. This was in keeping with the practice of the Catholic Church at the time. In the Protestant Reformation, some Protestants, such as Martin Luther, began to celebrate the Eucharist with both leavened and unleavened bread. Other Protestants, such as John Calvin, believed that the Eucharist should only be celebrated with unleavened bread. The Eucharist is an important part of many Christian denominations, and is considered to be a sacrament by most. It is a reminder of the Last Supper, and a way for Christians to remember and celebrate the life, death, and resurrection of Jesus Christ.

Is the Eucharist symbolic or literal?

The Easter holiday is a feast that commemorates the resurrection of Jesus Christ. The word "Easter" itself comes from a Germanic word meaning "springtime." The holiday falls on the first Sunday after the first full moon following the vernal equinox, making it a moveable feast. Christians believe that Jesus rose from the dead on the third day after his crucifixion. The Gospels of Matthew, Mark, and Luke all end with accounts of Jesus' resurrection. In the Gospel of John, Jesus predicts his own resurrection several times. On the night before his crucifixion, Jesus institutes the Eucharist, telling his disciples to "do this in remembrance" of him. The Eucharist, also known as Holy Communion, is a Christian sacrament in which bread and wine are consecrated and consumed. The word "Eucharist" comes from the Greek word for "thanksgiving." Christians believe that the Eucharist is a symbolic representation of the body and blood of Jesus Christ. There is debate among Christians as to whether the Eucharist is a symbolic or literal representation of Christ's body and blood. Some Christians believe that the Eucharist is a literal representation of Christ's body and blood. Others believe that the Eucharist is a symbolic representation of Christ's body and blood. Those who believe that the Eucharist is a literal representation of Christ's body and blood believe that the bread and wine are transformed into the actual body and blood of Christ. This belief is known as transubstantiation. The Catholic Church teaches that transubstantiation occurs during the Mass, when the priest says the words of Institution. Those who believe that the Eucharist is a symbolic representation of Christ's body and blood believe that the bread and wine represent the body and blood of Christ, but are not actually transformed into the body and blood of Christ. This belief is known as consubstantiation. Lutherans believe that Christ is present in the Eucharist, but not through transubstantiation. The debate over the nature of the Eucharist is not simply a matter of semantics. The belief that the Eucharist is a literal representation of Christ's body and blood has important implications for the Christian faith. Catholics believe that the Eucharist is the source and summit of their Christian life. They believe that receiving the Eucharist is essential for salvation. Protestants who believe that the Eucharist is a symbolic representation of Christ's body and blood do not believe that receiving the Eucharist is essential for salvation. They see the Eucharist as a means of remembering and celebrating what Christ has done for them. The debate over the nature of the Eucharist is not simply a matter of semantics. It is a debate that has important implications for the Christian faith.

What is the impact of Eucharist in life?

When Christians think about the impact of Eucharist in life, usually the first thing that comes to mind is how it brings us closer to God. The Eucharist is a sacrament that helps us to remember the self-sacrifice of Jesus Christ and to respond to God's love for us. It is a reminder that we are called to love one another and to put others before ourselves. The Eucharist is not just an individual act, but something that should be shared with other Christians. When we share the Eucharist, we are reminded that we are all part of the Body of Christ. We are all brothers and sisters in Christ, and we are all called to love one another. The Eucharist can have a profound impact on our lives if we let it. It can change the way we think about ourselves and about others. It can lead us to a deeper understanding of who God is and how much he loves us. It can help us to see the world in a new light and to respond to it in a new way.

How does the Eucharist influence daily life?

The eucharist is a central element of Catholic practice and daily life. It is a sacrament in which Catholics partake of the body and blood of Christ, symbolically consuming his flesh and blood to receive forgiveness and eternal life. The eucharist is a powerful reminder of the sacrifice Christ made for our salvation, and it is through this act of communion that we are able to receive the grace and strength to live a virtuous life. The eucharist has a profound impact on our daily lives, shaping our thoughts, actions, and decisions. It serves as a reminder of the great love that God has for us and of our need to continually turn to Him for guidance and strength. The eucharist challenges us to live out our faith in all aspects of our lives, and it gives us the grace to do so. When we receive the eucharist, we are reminded of the great sacrifice that Christ made for us. This prompts us to lives of sacrificial love, giving of ourselves in service to others. The eucharist challenges us to put our faith into action, to love our neighbor as ourselves. It urges us to reach out to those in need, to those who are suffering. The eucharist transforms us, making us more like Christ and leading us to lives of holiness. The eucharist is a source of strength and grace in our daily lives. It enables us to love more deeply, to forgive more readily, and to serve more selflessly. It challenges us to grow in holiness and to become more like Christ. The eucharist is a gift that keeps on giving, drawing us closer to God and to one another.

How the Eucharist influence your faith life?

The Eucharist is a sacrament or ordinance in Christianity. The Eucharist is also known as the Lord's Supper. It is a belief held by Christians that during the Eucharist, bread and wine are transformed into the body and blood of Jesus Christ. Christians believe that this happens through the power of the Holy Spirit. The Eucharist is an important part of Christian worship. It is seen as a way of remembering what Jesus did for humanity. It is also seen as a way of receiving Jesus into one's life. For many Christians, the Eucharist is a way of deepening their relationship with God. The Eucharist can have a profound effect on a person's faith life. It can be a moment of great spiritual intimacy with God. It can also be a time of great reflection on one's life and on the teachings of Jesus Christ. The Eucharist can also be a source of strength and comfort in times of difficulty. It can be a reminder that Jesus is with us always, even in the darkest of times. The Eucharist can help us to feel close to God and to know that we are never alone.

Why is the Eucharist the most powerful prayer?

The Eucharist is the most powerful prayer because it is the prayer that Jesus himself gave to us. When we celebrate the Eucharist, we are praying in the same way that Jesus prayed. We are asking God to bless the bread and wine, and to change them into Jesus' body and blood. We are asking God to give us the graces that we need to grow closer to him. The Eucharist is a powerful reminder of what Jesus did for us. He died for our sins, and he rose from the dead so that we could have eternal life. When we receive the Eucharist, we are receiving the body and blood of Christ. We are reminded that Jesus is with us always, and that he is the source of our strength and salvation. The Eucharist is a powerful intercession for us. When we receive Communion, we are asking Jesus to intercede for us with the Father. We are asking Jesus to pray for us, and to help us to grow closer to God. The Eucharist is a powerful expression of our love for God. When we receive Communion, we are telling God that we love him. We are telling him that we are willing to give ourselves to him completely. We are telling him that we want to be one with him. The Eucharist is the most powerful prayer because it is the prayer that Jesus himself gave to us. When we celebrate the Eucharist, we are praying in the same way that Jesus prayed. We are asking God to bless the bread and wine, and to change them into Jesus' body and blood. We are asking God to give us the graces that we need to grow closer to him. The Eucharist is a powerful reminder of what Jesus did for us. He died for our sins, and he rose from the dead so that we could have eternal life. When we receive the Eucharist, we are receiving the body and blood of Christ. We are reminded that Jesus is with us always, and that he is the source of our strength and salvation. The Eucharist is a powerful intercession for us. When we receive Communion, we are asking Jesus to intercede for us with the Father. We are asking Jesus to pray for us, and to help us to grow closer to God. The Eucharist is a powerful expression of our love for God. When we receive Communion, we are telling God that we love him. We are telling him that we are willing to give ourselves to him completely. We are telling him that we want to be one with him. The Eucharist is the most powerful prayer because it is the prayer that Jesus himself gave to us.

Do all Christians have the Eucharist?

The Eucharist, also known as Communion or the Lord's Supper, is a central sacrament in Christianity. The bread and wine become the body and blood of Christ, and Christians believe that they receive Jesus himself when they partake in the Eucharist. But not all Christians partake in this sacrament – some believe that the Eucharist is a symbolic act, and not a literal one. So the question remains – do all Christians have the Eucharist? The answer is no – not all Christians partake in the Eucharist. Some, like Catholics and Orthodox Christians, believe in the real presence of Christ in the Eucharist and partake in it regularly. Others, like Protestants, may believe that the Eucharist is a symbolic act, and thus don't partake in it. And still others, like the Coptic Christians of Egypt, don't believe in the real presence of Christ in the Eucharist but do consider it a spiritual mystery. So there is a wide range of beliefs among Christians when it comes to the Eucharist. But even though not all Christians partake in the Eucharist, it is still a central sacrament for many. Catholics and Orthodox Christians believe that the Eucharist is the source and summit of their faith – in other words, that it is the most important thing they do. For them, the Eucharist is a way to connect with Jesus on a very real and personal level. And for Protestants, even though they may not believe in the real presence of Christ in the Eucharist, it is still a meaningful and important symbol of their faith. So even though not all Christians have the Eucharist, it is still an important part of many Christian faith traditions.

The Easter holiday is a time for Christians to celebrate the resurrection of Jesus Christ. It is also a time for family and friends to get together and enjoy each other's company. Easter is a time to reflect on the past year and to look forward to the year ahead.

How is the Eucharist the greatest act of worship?

The Eucharist is the greatest act of worship because it is the most intimate way we can experience the presence of God. In the Eucharist, we not only remember the sacrifice of Jesus Christ on the cross, but we actually partake in the body and blood of Christ. This intimate act of Communion allows us to enter into a deep and personal relationship with God. During the Eucharist, we offer our entire selves to God – our body, mind, and spirit. We surrender ourselves to God completely, and in doing so, we experience the deepest possible level of worship. The Eucharist is a powerful reminder that we are created to be in relationship with God, and that our ultimate purpose is to love and serve Him. When we partake in the Eucharist, we are also participating in the New Covenant that God has made with us through the blood of Christ. This New Covenant is a sign of God's love for us, and it is our opportunity to respond to that love by committing ourselves to Him. The Eucharist is a powerful reminder of the many ways that God has blessed us, and it is our chance to show our gratitude to Him. The Eucharist is the highest form of worship because it is an act of total surrender to God. In the Eucharist, we lay down our own will and allow God to take control. We offer ourselves up to Him completely, and in doing so, we experience His presence in a deeply personal way. The Eucharist is a beautiful reminder of the deep love and commitment that we have to our Creator.

Who established the Eucharist and why?

The Eucharist is a central Christian sacrament in which believers consume bread and wine, symbolic of the body and blood of Christ. The ritual was established by Jesus during the Last Supper and is recorded in the Gospels. The exact origins of the Eucharist are unknown, but it is likely that it began as a Passover meal. As the early Church grew and spread throughout the world, the Eucharist became an important part of Christian worship. There are several theories as to why Jesus established the Eucharist. One is that it was a way to commemorate his sacrifice and to ensure that his followers would always remember him. Another is that it was a way to unite believers in a common experience of grace. Whatever the reasons, the Eucharist has been an essential part of the Christian faith for centuries. It is a sacred ritual that reminds us of the ultimate sacrifice of Jesus Christ and the great gift of grace that he offers to all who believe in him.

Is the Eucharist spiritual?

The Eucharist is a central mystery of the Christian faith. It is the enactment of Jesus' sacrifice on the cross, in which he offers his body and blood to God. The eucharist is a spiritual reality in which we are united with God and with one another. It is the source and summit of Christian life. The eucharist is a sacrament, an outward sign of an inward reality. When we partake of the eucharist, we are not simply partaking of bread and wine. We are partaking of the body and blood of Christ. This is a spiritual reality, not a physical one. Christ is present to us in a special way when we partake of the eucharist. The eucharist is a meal, but it is also so much more. It is a meal that nourishes us spiritually. When we partake of the eucharist, we are united with Christ and with one another. We become part of the Body of Christ. This is a spiritual reality, not a physical one. The eucharist is a sacrificial meal. When we partake of the eucharist, we are participating in the sacrifice of Christ. This is a spiritual reality, not a physical one. Christ died for our sins, and by partaking of the eucharist, we are uniting ourselves with his sacrifice. The eucharist is a mystery. It is a reality that is beyond our comprehension. We cannot understand it fully, but we can know that it is a sacred reality in which we are united with God.

Why is the Eucharist called the Most Blessed Sacrament?

The Eucharist is called the Most Blessed Sacrament because, in the words of the Catechism of the Catholic Church, "it is the source and summit of the Christian life." In other words, the Eucharist is the most important sacrament because it is the sacrament that brings us closest to Jesus Christ. The Eucharist is a sacrament that is unique in many ways. For one, it is the only sacrament that is celebrated in every single Mass. This means that, whenever we receive the Eucharist, we are receiving Jesus Christ himself. Additionally, the Eucharist is the only sacrament that can be received more than once. This is because, each time we receive the Eucharist, we are receiving Jesus' very body, blood, soul, and divinity. Because of all of these things, the Eucharist is rightly called the Most Blessed Sacrament. It is the sacrament that brings us into the closest possible communion with our Lord and Savior, and it is the sacrament that has the power to change our lives forever.

What makes the Holy Eucharist the greatest sacrament?

In the Catholic Church, the Holy Eucharist is the greatest of all the sacraments because it is the source and summit of the Christian life. The Eucharist is the real presence of Jesus Christ, who is the bread of life, and it is the only sacrament that allows us to receive him into our very bodies. The Eucharist is the sacrament of love. In the Eucharist, Jesus gives himself to us completely and unconditionally. He comes to us in the bread and wine, and he invites us to partake of his body and blood. This is a profound act of love, and it is an invitation to us to love in return. The Eucharist is also the sacrament of unity. In the Eucharist, we are called to come together as one body, to share in the one bread and one cup. This unity is a sign of the unity that we are called to have with each other and with God. The Eucharist is a powerful sign of hope. In the Eucharist, we remember that Jesus died and rose again, and we proclaim our hope that one day we will share in his risen life. The Eucharist is a sign that the love of God is stronger than death, and that nothing can separate us from his love. The Eucharist is a mystery that is beyond our human understanding. In the Eucharist, we receive the very body and blood of Jesus Christ, who is the Son of God. This is a mystery that we cannot fully comprehend, but it is a mystery that we can believe and receive with faith. The Eucharist is a great gift that we receive from God. It is a gift that we cannot earn or deserve, but it is a gift that we are offered freely by God's grace. The Eucharist is a sign of God's love for us, and it is a sign of our desire to return that love.

It is clear that Easter is a very important holiday for Christians around the world. For many, it is a time to come together and celebrate the resurrection of Jesus Christ. For others, it is a time to reflect on their own personal beliefs. No matter what your perspective is, Easter is a time to rejoice and be thankful for what we have.

Why do Protestants not believe in Eucharist?

There are a few different reasons why Protestants do not believe in the Eucharist. One reason is that they see it as a Catholic tradition and not something that is rooted in scripture. Protestants also tend to believe that the Eucharist is not a necessity for salvation and that it is not a necessary part of worship. Additionally, some Protestants believe that the Eucharist is a man-made tradition and not something that was instituted by Jesus Christ.

Are Eucharist and Mass the same?

The Easter Eucharist, also known as the Paschal Eucharist, is a Christian sacrament commemorating the resurrection of Jesus Christ. It is also sometimes called the Mass. The Easter Eucharist is considered to be one of the most important events in the Christian calendar, and is celebrated by Christians around the world. There is some debate amongst Christians as to whether the Easter Eucharist and the Mass are the same thing. Some believe that they are two separate events, while others believe that the Mass is simply a more formal version of the Easter Eucharist. Those who believe that the Easter Eucharist and the Mass are two separate events typically argue that the Mass is a more solemn and formal event, while the Easter Eucharist is a more joyful and celebratory occasion. They may also point to the fact that the Mass is typically celebrated in a church, while the Easter Eucharist can be celebrated anywhere. Those who believe that the Easter Eucharist and the Mass are the same event typically argue that the Mass is simply a more formal version of the Easter Eucharist. They may point to the fact that both events commemorated the resurrection of Jesus Christ, and that both involve the sharing of bread and wine. The truth is, there is no right or wrong answer to this question. It is a matter of personal belief. Whatever your belief, the important thing is to celebrate the Easter Eucharist in a way that is meaningful to you and brings you joy.

Why do some Christians not celebrate the Eucharist?

There are some Christians who do not celebrate the Eucharist, believing that it is not a Scriptural practice. The Eucharist, also known as Holy Communion, is the sharing of bread and wine by Christians in remembrance of Jesus' sacrifice on the cross. While the exact origins of the Eucharist are debated, the practice is thought to have started with the Last Supper, as recorded in the Gospels. There are a number of reasons why some Christians do not believe in celebrating the Eucharist. One reason is that they do not believe in the doctrine of transubstantiation, which is the belief that the bread and wine actually become the body and blood of Christ. Another reason is that they believe that the Eucharist is a Catholic practice, and that Protestants should not participate in it. Additionally, some Christians believe that the Eucharist is not necessary for salvation, and that it is simply a reminder of what Christ has already done for us. Whatever the reason, Christians who do not celebrate the Eucharist are still part of the Body of Christ. And while they may not participate in this particular practice, they still hold to the central tenants of the faith, including believing in the death and resurrection of Jesus Christ.

Who is allowed Eucharist?

The Eucharist, also known as Holy Communion, is a Christian rite that is considered a sacrament in most churches. In order to receive the Eucharist, one must be a baptized Christian. There are some denominations of Christianity, such as the Catholic Church, that require one to be in a state of grace in order to receive the Eucharist. This means that one must be free from mortal sin. Some churches, such as the Anglican Communion, do not have this requirement. In order to receive the Eucharist, one must believe that it is the body and blood of Jesus Christ. This is known as the Real Presence. The Real Presence is a doctrine that is held by most, but not all, Christians. Those who do not believe in the Real Presence are known as 21st Century Friends or Free Christians. The Eucharist is not just a meal, but a sacred act. It is a way of expressing our faith and our belief in the Real Presence. When we partake in the Eucharist, we are remembering the sacrifice that Jesus made for us on the cross. We are also proclaiming our belief in the Resurrection. The Eucharist is a way of uniting ourselves with Jesus Christ and with the rest of the Christian community. The Eucharist is a sacred and special sacrament. It is a way of expression our faith and our love for Jesus Christ. It is a reminder of the sacrifice that he made for us on the cross. It is also a reminder of the hope that we have in the Resurrection. The Eucharist is a way of bringing us closer to Jesus Christ and to the rest of the Christian community.

The Easter holiday is a time for family, fun, and, of course, food. From traditional Easter eggs to ham and lamb, there are many delicious dishes to enjoy on this special day. Whether you're attending an Easter brunch or dinner, or simply enjoying a meal at home with your loved ones, Easter is a great time to enjoy good food and company.

the religious colours of easter

Easter is a religious holiday that has been celebrated for centuries. The holiday has many different traditions and meanings, but the one thing that remains the same is the importance of the colors used during Easter. The colors of Easter represent hope, new life, and rebirth. They are a reminder that Spring is on its way and that the world is renewing itself. The colors of Easter also remind us of the sacrifice that was made for us and the hope that we have because of it. The most common colors used during Easter are white, yellow, and purple. White represents purity, innocence, and new beginnings. Yellow represents joy, happiness, and life. Purple represents royalty, majesty, and Lent. Lent is the 40 day period of fasting and prayer that leads up to Easter. It is a time of reflection and repentance. The color purple is used to remind us of the sacrifices made during Lent and the hope that we have because of them. The colors of Easter are a reminder of the hope that we have because of the sacrifice of Jesus Christ. He died for our sins so that we may have eternal life. The colors of Easter are a reminder of the new life that we have in Christ. They are a reminder that no matter what happens in this life, we have hope because Christ has conquered death.

What started as a pagan holiday commemorating the return of spring has become, for many, a day to celebrate the resurrection of Jesus Christ. Whether you believe in the religious aspects of Easter or not, there's no denying that it's a day that has come to mean a lot to a lot of people. For some, it's a time to get together with family and friends and enjoy a traditional Easter feast. For others, it's a day to reflect on their faith and what it means to them. No matter what Easter means to you, there's no doubt that it's a special day.

Have Questions / Comments?

This book was designed to cover as much as possible but I know I have probably missed something, or some new amazing discovery that has just come out.

If you notice something missing or have a question that I failed to answer, please get in touch and let me know. If I can, I will email you an answer and also update the book so others can also benefit from it.

Thanks For Being Incredible :)

Submit Your Questions / Comments At:

https://BornIncredible.com/questions/

Get Another Book Free

We love writing and have produced a huge number of books.

For being one of our amazing readers, we would love to offer you another book we have created, 100% free.

To claim this limited time special offer, simply go to the site below and enter your name and email address.

You will then receive one of my great books, direct to your email account, 100% free!

https://BornIncredible.com/ free-book-offer/

Also by Emma J. Lee

Easter: Everything You Need To Know About Lent and Easter

CPSIA information can be obtained
at www.ICGtesting.com
Printed in the USA
LVHW032017220323
742311LV00014B/1324

9 781776 969982